Belgium

Text by George McDonald
Updated by Derek Blyth
Managing Editor: Tony Halliday

Berlitz POCKET GUIDE

Belgium

First Edition (2003)
Updated 2006

PHOTOGRAPHY:
Belgian Tourist Office – Brussels & Wallonia 9, 73, 76, 79, 85, 91; Berlitz 38; Pete Bennett 3TL, 3CR, 6, 22, 24, 25, 26, 27, 29, 30, 31, 34, 35, 36, 43; Jerry Dennis 53; Annabel Elston 65, 71; Tony Halliday 14, 16, 52, 54, 58, 92; Mark Read 18, 33, 87, 88, 96, 97, 99; Georgie Scott 1, 3CL, 10, 40, 44, 45, 46, 49, 51, 57, 60, 61, 62, 63, 66, 67, 68, 72, 74, 77, 78, 79, 80, 82, 89, 93, 101; George Taylor 8
Cover Photograph: Powerstock

CONTACTING THE EDITORS
Every effort has been made to provide accurate information in this publication, but changes are inevitable. The publisher cannot be responsible for any resulting loss, inconvenience or injury. We would appreciate it if readers would call our attention to any errors or outdated information by contacting Berlitz Publishing, PO Box 7910, London SE1 1WE, England.
Fax: (44) 20 7403 0290;
e-mail: berlitz@apaguide.co.uk
www.berlitzpublishing.com

The resort town of Spa, where people still come to take the waters (page 78)

Jan van Eyck's altarpiece in St Bavo's cathedral, at the heart of medieval Ghent (page 51)

Antwerp Cathedral with its spire soaring high above a statue of Rubens (page 43)

TOP TEN ATTRACTIONS

Le Cygne (The Swan), one of the historic guildhalls overlooking the famous Grand-Place in Brussels (page 23)

The elegant resort of De Haan, graced by villas from the *belle époque* (page 58)

The rivers of the Ardennes offer plenty of choice for canoeists of all abilities (page 84)

Butte du Lion, standing guard over the Waterloo battlefield (page 38)

Magnificent gardens at the Château d'Annevoie in the Meuse Valley (page 72)

Grottes de Han, a spectacular complex of caves, through which flows the River Lesse (page 77)

The perfectly preserved medieval town of Bruges, a highlight of any trip to Belgium (page 52)

CONTENTS

A ➤ in the text denotes a highly recommended sight

Fact Sheets

INTRODUCTION

Belgium is a land of secrets. Many of these are 'hidden' in plain sight, but to uncover others you need to be prepared to dig a little, to get below the surface.

The neighbouring countries make the most of their relative homogeneity to present a reasonably unified picture to the outside world. Visitors know roughly what they're going to get when they travel to France, Germany, Holland and England. But Belgium?

An astonishing degree of diversity is contained within the borders of this small, densely populated land. The country straddles one of Europe's age-old, fundamental lines of division – between the Germanic north and the Latin south – splitting the country across its waist into Dutch-speaking Flemish and French-speaking Walloon halves. Forget about unity. Politically and administratively this combination generates stresses and strains and a degree of absurdity. But so far as language, history, culture, cuisine and tradition go, it's like getting two countries for the price of one.

False Modesty

Despite this, the Belgians are not very good at blowing their own trumpet. They permit the French to claim the cuisine award, even though Belgium has more Michelin star restaurants per capita; the Germans to grab the best-beer label, despite Belgium's 500 remarkably varied beers; and the Dutch to preen themselves as the land of cheese, when the Belgians have 300 artisanal varieties to counter Edam and Gouda.

Perhaps the most puzzling accusation that's often made is that Belgium is 'boring'. Diversity can be its own reward, taking care of most of that misconception all by itself. Anyone who needed a lot of persuasion could do no better than to visit one of the costumed pre-Lenten carnivals that erupt with fervour across the land.

The territory that is now Belgium has been coveted and fought over for thousands of years. Today, the nation that once was criss-crossed by foreign invaders is traversed by millions of visitors, most of whom are on their way to holidays elsewhere in Europe. But more and more travellers are learning the secrets of Belgium.

Belgium's Regions and Attractions

Belgium is just 327km (200 miles) across, but doesn't seem small on the ground. Some 10 million people live in its 30,500 sq km (12,100 sq miles), a population density of 330 per sq km (825 per sq mile), among the highest in the world.

Brussels-Capital region, with a population of 1 million, is carved out of the low hills and swampy valleys of Brabant in the middle of the country. The hub of the nation's transport, Brussels itself labours under the weight of its 'capital of Europe' burden, but compensates with outstanding restaurants and cafés, a legacy of art nouveau architecture, and that cheeky little symbol of the city, *Manneken-Pis*.

Art nouveau at the Horta Museum in Brussels

Flanders *(Vlaanderen)* in the north, with a population of about 5.7 million, comprises the provinces of Antwerp, East Flanders, Flemish Brabant, Limburg and West Flanders. It is mostly flat, the only real exception being a range of low hills around Ronse and Geraardsbergen called the Flemish Ardennes. Behind

Bouillon Castle in the Ardennes

the coastal sand-dunes and along the Scheldt and other rivers is reclaimed land, or polders. The city of Antwerp is Europe's second port, after Rotterdam. In addition, Flanders has the art cities of Bruges and Ghent, as well as Ostend and the North Sea coast, Ypres (Ieper) and the battlefields of World War I, and the heathland of the Kempen.

With some 3.3 million inhabitants, Wallonia *(Wallonie)* covers the French-speaking south and comprises the provinces of Hainaut, Liège, Luxembourg, Namur and Walloon Brabant, including Waterloo and historic Tournai. Some of its population continues to speak the ancient Walloon dialect, and about 67,000 people in the East Cantons *(Ostkantone)* speak German. In the Ardennes, Wallonia has one of northwest Europe's most rugged regions, the eroded remnant of a mountain range between the scenic River Meuse valley and Germany.

Tourist information offices, from the national right down to the local level, are very helpful. All of them can provide maps,

Students in Leuven

brochures, leaflets, guides, advice, accommodation information and reservations. You can cycle in the flat polders of Flanders and in the steep hills of the Ardennes, 'sail' sand yachts at De Panne, scale the cliffs along the River Meuse, ski in the Ardennes in winter and with a bit of fortune skate on the canals of Bruges. Try riding your own *hofkar* (horse-and-carriage) in the Kempen, go horse-riding in the Forêt de Soignes outside Brussels, birdwatch at coastal mud-flats, sail at the coast and on lakes, or fish and canoe in the rivers of the Ardennes. Going off the beaten track affords plenty of surprises, particularly in isolated areas such as the Ardennes, the Kempen, West Flanders and the south of Hainaut.

Politics and People

Since gaining its independence from the Netherlands in 1830–1, Belgium has been a constitutional monarchy. The current sovereign is King Albert II, who came to the throne in 1993, and it is supposed that his son Prince Philippe will eventually succeed him. There are two houses of Parliament: the Senate and the Chamber of Representatives. Constitutional changes in recent times have boosted the importance of the regions – Brussels-Capital, Flanders and Wallonia – and the language communities – French, Dutch and German – at the expense of the central government, which now basically handles defence, foreign relations, social security and national economic policy, while the regions have virtual autonomy over their own affairs.

From the 19th century up to about the 1960s, Wallonia's heavy industries were the dominant power in the economy. Since then, Flanders has proved more adept at attracting and creating the new high-tech and service industries. The presence of governments – European, Belgian and Flemish – diplomats, and international organisations such as NATO goes a long way towards explaining Brussels' prosperity.

The majority of the population is Roman Catholic, and the virtues of community cohesion in work and play make up much of what it is to be Belgian. Tradition and family life are important and people take their work and their pleasures seriously. Eating and drinking in Belgium are mostly hearty events and form an important part of life. The country's cuisine is justly famous, both for its quality and its quantity. Not for nothing is the Belgian way of life described as 'Burgundian'.

Belgians have a quiet sense of pride in their achievements and in their history – Julius Caesar praised their resistance to his campaign of conquest, and for a time in the 15th and 16th centuries Belgium was the seat of the powerful Burgundian and Habsburg empires. And the contribution of Belgian artists to medieval, Renaissance and modern art movements is unquestioned. Equally important is pride in their roots, be they Flemish, Walloon or German.

In any language, it adds up to *vive la différence*.

> **Today's Belgians help to keep the past alive by maintaining guilds and societies dedicated to all manner of historical events and traditions: musketeers, archers, crossbowmen, fanfares, Napoleonic re-enactors, folkloric festivals, hunts, carnivals, saints, dances, civic and religious processions, beers, gins and local gastronomic specialities.**

A BRIEF HISTORY

The nation only came into being in 1830, but the lands that form Belgium can lay claim to a long and distinguished history, even if for most of that time they have been a fiefdom of other kingdoms and empires. From the second half of the 1st millennium BC, a group of Celtic peoples, called the Belgae by the Romans, lived in this northern part of Gaul. Julius Caesar conquered the Belgae between 57 and 54BC, though not without effective objections from the natives, including the defeat of two legions by the tribal leader Ambiorix in 54BC. Caesar wrote: 'Of all the peoples of Gaul, the Belgae are the bravest.'

When Rome's frontier moved to the River Rhine, Belgium became a peaceful backwater. Settlements such as Tournai and Tongeren grew into towns. The empire's decay from the 4th century AD onwards allowed Germanic tribes such as the Franks to break in, plunder, and eventually to settle in the region. When the Rhine barrier ruptured in 406, Roman control in Belgium came to an end. The Franks under the fierce King Childeric set up their first capital at Tournai, but Childeric's son Clovis moved it to Paris.

In 861, Count Baldwin I of Flanders, known as the 'Iron Arm', eloped with the daughter of the king of France, Charles the Bald. When Charles moved to chastise his son-in-law, Baldwin responded with a threat to ally with the Normans against him. So Charles was forced to swallow his pride and accept the new family arrangements.

The Franks

The Franks ruled over present-day Belgium, France and parts of Germany and Holland. In 768, Charlemagne established a unified Frankish kingdom and went on to found a European empire, culminating in his coronation by Pope Leo III in 800 as Emperor of the West. On Charlemagne's death in 814, his empire was divided between his three grandsons. The division left a narrow strip of northwest Europe that included the Low Countries (Belgium, the Netherlands and Luxembourg). Its position between the French and German nations, set the stage for Belgium's turbulent destiny right up to World War II.

Antwerp's Steen fortress dates from the 13th century

The area was under the nominal rule of French and German kings, but real power was in the hands of local nobles, who did their best to weaken the hold over them by the neighbouring feudal kingdoms. Among these overlords were the counts of Flanders, the dukes of Brabant and the prince-bishops of Liège. Some of them, wealthier than their rulers, were able to negotiate charters of autonomous rights for towns in exchange for taxes and providing military assistance.

The cloth towns of Flanders flourished in the 12th and 13th centuries. Bruges monopolised the market in English wool and was the richest town north of the Alps thanks to its trade connections with Europe, the Middle East and the Orient. International banking houses made the town their headquarters and the Baltic-based Hanseatic League set up a *kontor* (trading station) there. Ghent developed into the largest town in western Europe, and Ypres (Ieper) prospered too.

France continually tried to reassert control. A high point in the struggle of Flanders against French domination came in

Medieval life as depicted in Bruges Town Hall

1302, when a ragtag army of Flemish peasants slaughtered the French armoured knights at the Battle of the Golden Spurs.

Burgundians and Habsburgs

In 1384, Flanders became part of the Burgundian lands, when Duke Philip the Bold of Burgundy inherited the title of Count of Flanders through his wife. He administered his possessions in Burgundy from Bruges and was a patron of the arts, his court renowned for its splendour. A combination of dynastic marriages and military force allowed Philip's successors as duke – John the Fearless, Philip the Good and Charles the Bold – to extend Burgundian rule across most of the Low Countries. Brussels was the duchy's capital.

Charles's death in 1477 precipitated a French invasion. His daughter, Mary of Burgundy, in need of a powerful protector, married the Habsburg Prince Maximilian of Austria, the future Holy Roman Emperor. Mary died after falling from her horse while hunting in 1482, but through her marriage and the subsequent match between her son, Philip the Handsome, and Joanna the Mad of Spain, the Low Countries came to be joined with Spain and with the Habsburg's own Austrian possessions in the hands of her famous grandson, the emperor Charles V.

Born in Ghent in 1500 and appointed King of Spain in 1516 and Holy Roman Emperor in 1519, Charles continued a policy of favouring Antwerp and Brussels over the cloth towns of Flanders, which speeded the decline of Bruges and Ghent. Charles's reign is recalled every summer in the *Ommegang*, a colourful procession in the Grand-Place in Brussels.

Spanish Rule

The seeds of the Reformation, which stressed the rights of individuals to read and interpret the Word of God for themselves and questioned the control exercised by State and Church in alliance, were sown with the issue by the German monk Martin Luther of his *95 Theses* at Wittenberg in 1517.

The Noose Bearers of Ghent

Charles V, Holy Roman Emperor and King of Spain, ruler of the Habsburg lands in the Low Countries, Burgundy, Austria, Germany, Italy, Spain and the Americas, was born at Ghent's Prinsenhof on 24 February, 1500, and baptised in St Bavo's Cathedral.

Despite their city having been his birthplace, Charles never forgave the people of Ghent for their treasonous behaviour in the 1530s when they launched a public protest against heavy taxation and a collapsing economy. He had the ringleaders executed and forced the city's dignitaries to appear before him, on their knees, bareheaded and each with a noose around his neck, and to beg him for mercy.

To this day, the annual procession of the *Stropendragers* (Noose Bearers), recalls the humiliation Charles forced upon the city.

With the emergence of Luther, and later of Calvin, pressure for reform turned into outright revolt. Protestantism was born. The Low Countries were particularly receptive to the new ideas, as rich merchants chafed against the restrictions of a rigidly hierarchical social system, and the artisanal guilds had always resented any royal authority.

Charles V abdicated in 1555 in favour of his son Philip II of Spain, a fanatical Catholic who tried to crush Protestantism in the Low Countries and reinstate the authority of the Catholic Church. In 1565, a year of widespread famine, Protestant workers and peasants ran riot through Brussels, Bruges, Ghent, Antwerp and other towns, looting and destroying churches in an orgy of violence known as the Iconoclastic Fury.

Charles V, Holy Roman Emperor, in the Palace of the Liberty of Bruges

Frightened for their own positions, the nobility sided with Philip, and in 1567 Philip sent Spanish troops under the brutal Duke of Alba to the Low Countries. Full-scale military conflict broke out, before a short-lived period of peace and religious freedom was instigated by the Pacification of Ghent, a treaty signed in 1576. Two years later Philip renewed the war by sending a fresh army under the Duke of Parma, which reconquered the south – corresponding more or less to present-day Belgium – while leaving most of the north in the hands of the Dutch rebels.

Austrian Rule

The Spanish line of the Habsburgs ended in 1700 when Charles II died without an heir. To prevent the French royal house taking over in Spain, Austria and other European powers declared war in 1701. By the treaty that ended the War of the Spanish Succession in 1713, Belgium was handed over to the Austrian Habsburgs as the Austrian Netherlands.

Under Archduchess Maria Theresa of Austria, Belgium prospered from subsidised trade. During this period, architecture, lacemaking and art flourished. But distribution of the new wealth was limited mainly to the aristocracy and the merchants, while the majority of the population barely managed to scrape a living.

Maria Theresa was succeeded in 1780 by her son Joseph II. Although he instituted several enlightened, secularising reforms, his lack of consultation and his 'top down' approach created widespread resentment. In 1790, rebels proclaimed the United States of Belgium, and won recognition from Britain and the Netherlands. The fledgling nation was defeated a year later by the forces of the new Austrian emperor, Leopold II.

French Rule

In 1794, Republican France invaded and occupied Belgium, which later became part of Napoleon's empire. The country was divided into *départements* along French lines and the old absolutist system of government was removed. Unjust aspects of Church, State and taxation were reformed or abolished. There was rapid and subsidised industrialisation, with France being the main market for Belgian manufactured goods.

After Napoleon's final defeat, at Waterloo near Brussels in 1815, the Congress of Vienna perpetuated Belgium's subjuga-

**Colonne du Congrès in Brussels,
commemorating independence**

tion by giving control of the country to the Dutch House of Orange and joining it to the Netherlands.

Independence

The successful revolution against Dutch rule in 1830 created a free Belgian state, which took its name from the Belgae, the Celtic tribes who had fought against Rome nearly 2,000 years earlier. In 1831, the London Conference recognised the independence and neutrality of Belgium. Prince Leopold, of the German house of Saxe-Coburg, was crowned king of the Belgians as Leopold I.

Through the 19th century, Belgium modernised and industrialised. Yet tensions between the two linguistic groups within the country, French-speakers and Dutch-speakers, became more obvious as persistent social difficulties remained unresolved. Predominantly Dutch-speaking and increasingly prosperous Flanders began to agitate for independence from French-speaking Wallonia.

Instead of attending to the problems of his country, the new king, Leopold II, who acceded to the throne in 1865, devoted most of his time to personal interests, including a mania for grandiose architectural projects and his private commercial dealings in the Belgian Congo, a colony acquired in 1881.

The World Wars

Leopold was succeeded in 1909 by his nephew, Albert I, and it was during his reign that World War I gripped Belgium, from 1914 to 1918. The German army invaded, despite the country's neutrality, and occupied most of it, forcing the king to retreat to a narrow strip of unoccupied land. His staunch resistance to the invader earned him the sobriquet 'Soldier King'. Some of the bloodiest battles of the war took place around Ypres (Ieper) in Flanders. Germany's defeat won Belgium considerable reparations and new territory in the east, along the German frontier.

After the war, reforms were introduced aimed at creating equality between the Flemish and Walloons, but with the rise of fascist tendencies in both communities, relations grew more antagonistic. In 1940, Nazi Germany launched its *blitzkrieg* through Belgium and occupied the country in just three weeks. This time there was no heroic resistance on the part of the king, Leopold III, who had acceded to the throne in 1934 following the death of Albert in a climbing accident. A resistance movement formed, and included an underground network to protect Belgium's Jewish community. However, the behaviour of the king, who was eager to accommodate the invaders (or to secure concessions for the populace, as his supporters argued), caused much controversy after the war.

In Flanders Fields

In Flanders fields the poppies blow/Between the crosses, row on row/That mark our place; and in the sky/The larks, still bravely singing, fly/Scarce heard amid the guns below/We are the dead. Short days ago/We lived, felt dawn, saw sunset glow/Loved, and were loved. And now we lie/In Flanders fields
Lt Colonel John McCrae, 1915

In 1950, the people voted by a narrow margin to invite the king home from exile, but Leopold chose to abdicate in favour of his son Baudouin I.

Modern Belgium

In 1948, Benelux, an economic union between Belgium, the Netherlands and Luxembourg, was formed, and in 1957 Belgium co-founded the European Economic Community, the forerunner of today's European Union. Brussels, a seat of European empires in the past, now hosts the European Commission and the Parliament of the European Union, and is officially recognised as the 'capital of Europe'.

Internal politics since the end of World War II have centred on the continuing friction between the Flemings and Walloons. In 1977, the three federal regions of Brussels-Capital, Flanders and Wallonia were established in the hope that more self-determination would ease the tensions between the groups. In 1989, regional governments were created, and in 1994 a new constitution was adopted, establishing Belgium as a federal state.

While many people predicted the imminent break-up of Belgium, the country has so far weathered every crisis. Its survival has been secured by the immense popularity of King Albert II, who came to the throne in 1993 following the sudden death of his brother Baudouin. When Belgium celebrated its 175th anniversary in 2005, it was clear from the scale of the celebrations that this was a country with a firm sense of its own unique identity.

European Parliament building

Historical Landmarks

circa 300BC Celtic tribes occupy territory that is now Belgium.
57–54BC Julius Caesar conquers the Belgian tribes.
5th century AD Franks conquer Belgium; Tournai is their capital.
768 Charlemagne crowned King of the Franks.
861 Baldwin 'Iron Arm' is Count of Flanders.
979 Foundation of Brussels.
1302 Flanders defeats France at Battle of the Golden Spurs.
1419 Philip the Good of Burgundy becomes Count of Flanders.
1477 Mary of Burgundy marries Austrian Prince Maximilian.
1519 Charles V crowned Holy Roman Emperor.
1531 Brussels becomes the capital of the Spanish Netherlands.
1555 Charles abdicates; Philip II of Spain succeeds.
1567–79 Religious wars in Low Countries.
1576 Pacification of Ghent aims to permit religious freedom.
1713 Treaty of Utrecht cedes Belgium to Austria.
1790 Proclamation of United States of Belgium.
1794 France invades and annexes Belgium.
1815 Congress of Vienna cedes Belgium to Netherlands.
1830 Belgian revolution and independence.
1914–18 World War I; Germany occupies most of Belgium.
1940–4 World War II; Germany occupies Belgium.
1948 Benelux customs union formed.
1949 Belgium joins NATO.
1957 Belgium is founding member of the EEC.
1959 European Commission located in Brussels.
1967 NATO moves its HQ to Brussels.
1977 Establishment of three federal regions.
1989 Regional governments created.
1993 Albert II succeeds Baudouin I as king.
1994 Belgium re-established, as a federal state.
2002 Euro introduced as Belgian currency.
2005 Belgium celebrates 175th anniversary of independence.

WHERE TO GO

BRUSSELS (BRUXELLES/BRUSSEL)

Brussels, with a population of a million, sits astride the frontier between Dutch-speaking Flanders and French-speaking Wallonia, but is a federal region of Belgium in its own right. Capital of Belgium, capital of Europe and capital of Flanders, the city has become synonymous with bureaucracy. Yet this is no spiritless centre of government. The soul of an older Brussels still beats strongly, particularly in the many restaurants and cafés, and the adjective 'Burgundian' can still be used to characterise its lifestyle.

Grand-Place

The historic **Grand-Place** at the heart of Brussels, a UNESCO World Heritage Site, is among Europe's most handsome squares. Its 17th-century guildhalls, in Flemish Renaissance and Italianate-Flemish styles, were built in the space of a few years after

> In 979, the Duke of Lorraine occupied a castle at a marshy agricultural settlement known as Bruocsella (Brussels). This is said to be the foundation date of the future capital of Europe.

a 1695 French artillery bombardment had destroyed their predecessors. This gives the ensemble a remarkable unity, though there is plenty of diversity of architectural and decorative detail.

Before you notice these, your gaze is likely to be drawn by the magnificent **Hôtel de Ville** (Town Hall; open for guided tours Apr–Sept: Tues and Wed 3.15pm, Sun 10.45am and 12.15pm; Oct–Mar: Tues and Wed 3.15pm; admission fee) on the west side. Begun in 1401 and completed in 1459, this

The Hôtel de Ville (Town Hall) on the Grand-Place in Brussels

The Maison du Roi fronts one side of the Grand-Place

late-Gothic masterpiece has intricately carved façades, and an off-centre belfry that soars 96m (312ft) and is surmounted by a gilded statue of the city's patron saint, the Archangel Michael. The city council convenes in a mahogany-lined chamber within, hung with tapestries depicting scenes from the life of Clovis, King of the Franks.

Across the cobblestoned square is the almost equally impressive, neo-Gothic **Maison du Roi** (King's House), from 1887. This houses not a king but the **Musée de la Ville de Bruxelles** (Brussels Municipal Museum; open Tues–Sun 10am–5pm; admission fee), in which you can trace the city's development from a Dark Ages village to the capital of Europe, and view some of the 600 different costumes of *Manneken-Pis (see page 26).*

Most of the guildhalls now house private apartments, cafés, restaurants, shops, a disco, banks and a hotel, but somehow they have managed to retain an elegant air. Among the notable guildhalls, the **Maisons des Ducs de Brabant** (House of the Dukes of Brabant) on the southern side – it's actually six guildhalls under a single roof – is one of the most beautiful. Dating from 1698, its façade is embellished with busts of 19 dukes. In the hall at No. 13, the **Musée du Chocolat** (Chocolate Museum) celebrates Belgium's passion for handmade pralines.

A gable that resembles the stern of a 17th-century ship decorates **Le Cornet** (The Horn) at No. 6, which was the Boatmen's Guildhall. Karl Marx worked on *The Communist Manifesto* at No. 9, **Le Cygne** (The Swan), once the Butchers' Guildhall and now a restaurant. In **Le Pigeon** (The Dove) at No. 26–27, an equally fiery exiled writer, Victor Hugo, composed invective aimed at French Emperor Napoleon III until the authorities told him to leave town. The Belgian brewers' trade association and their guild, the Knights of the Mash Staff, still occupy the **Maison des Brasseurs** (House of the Brewers) at No. 10, and the **Musée de la Brasserie** (Museum of Brewing; open daily 10am–5pm; admission fee), offers an insight into past brewing methods and a taste the finished product from today.

The Old Centre

The Grand-Place is at the focus of a circle of places of interest. Beginning at its southwestern corner, the **Musée du Costume et de la Dentelle** (Costume and Lace Museum; open Mon, Tues, Thur and Fri 10am–12.30pm, and 1.30–5pm; Sat–Sun 2–5pm; admission fee) in Rue de la Violette contains costumes and lace from the 17th

Exhibit at the Costume and Lace Museum

century onwards. At the corner of Rue du Chêne and Rue de l'Etuve is *Manneken-Pis*, that irreverent symbol of Brussels, a sculpture-fountain of a little boy exuberantly doing *pee-pee*. It dates from 1619 (but this is a replica, cast from a mould made from the damaged original). Occasionally, 'Little Julian' can be seen wearing one of his 600 costumes, among them a uniform of the Welsh Guards (who liberated Brussels in 1944), a Belgian national football strip and an Elvis costume, which are displayed at the Musée de la Ville de Bruxelles *(see page 24)*.

The ornate, neoclassical **Bourse** (Stock Exchange) from 1873 in Rue Henri Maus is surrounded by fine cafés and restaurants. In a busy part of town, the adjacent 11th-century Romanesque **Eglise St-Nicolas** (Church of St Nicholas) is a quietly spiritual oasis. Refurbished in Gothic style in the 14th century and rebuilt several times since, the handsome little church still shows traces of its original rough construction.

Belgium's 1830 revolution against Dutch rule began at the neoclassical **Théâtre Royal de la Monnaie** (Royal Mint Theatre) in Place de la Monnaie, when an opera singer launched into a patriotic aria and the fired-up audience stormed into the streets. The Monnaie is still the city's main venue for

Manneken-Pis

opera and ballet. Just off adjacent Rue Neuve, the 18th-century, neoclassical **Place des Martyrs** was later dedicated to the patriots killed in the revolution. A central crypt holds their remains.

Uphill in Rue des Sables, the colourful **Centre Belge de la Bande Dessinée** (Belgian Comic-Strip Centre; open Tues–Sun 10am–6pm; admission fee) – known as

Inside the Belgian Comic-Strip Centre

the 'CéBéBéDé' for short – displays mementoes and collections of comic strips from around the world, including Belgium's own Tintin, Lucky Luke, Thorgal and more.

Although raised to cathedral status only in 1961, the magnificent Gothic **Cathédrale des Saints-Michel-et-Gudule** (open Apr–Sept: daily 7am–7pm; Oct–Mar: daily 7am–6pm; cathedral free, admission fee to crypt), across Boulevard de Berlaimont, was begun in 1226 and is fully the equal of Europe's great cathedrals. Its white stone façade and soaring twin spires offset a rather plain interior, whose primary embellishment is the 16th-century stained-glass windows donated by Emperor Charles V.

Back towards the Grand-Place, the **Galeries Royales St-Hubert** (St Hubert Royal Galleries) is an enclosed 'mall' of three connecting galleries, from 1847, in Italian neo-Renaissance style, containing stylish and expensive shops, restaurants and cafés.

The Lower Town

Around **Place Ste-Catherine**, the original heart of Brussels was a group of marshy islets in the River Senne – these have long been joined together and in the 19th century the river was covered over. The canalside harbour where fishing boats once unloaded their catches has been filled in and its place taken by an ornamental pool and fountain, but the **Marché-aux-Poissons** (Fish Market) is still here. Adjacent Quai-aux-Briques and Quai-au-Bois-à-Brûler are lined with seafood restaurants. Joseph Poelaert, the architect of the Palais de Justice, designed the 19th-century **Eglise Ste-Catherine** (St Catherine's Church) in the square.

Royal Road

Running in virtually a straight north–south line east of the city centre, Rue de la Régence and Rue Royale link many notable sights. Beginning at the south end of Rue de la Régence, the vast, domed neoclassical **Palais de Justice** (Palace of Justice) from 1883 stands on a hill that was the site of the public gallows.

Brussels' metro stations are the setting for works of – literally – underground art. Top Belgian artists, including Roger Somville, Paul Delvaux and Emile Dubrunfaut, have created murals, sculptures and installations to amuse, challenge and entertain. Viewing this 'gallery' could not be simpler: buy a one-day metro pass and go.

Place du Grand-Sablon is a square with a reputation for high quality and fancy prices in its private art galleries and antiques shops and at the weekend antiques market, as well as in its chic cafés and restaurants. Some of the latter have street terraces, but the traffic detracts from the overall experience. The **Eglise Notre-Dame-du-Sablon** (Church of Our

Lady of the Sablon) – its proper name is Notre-Dame-des-Victoires (Our Lady of Victories) – dates from the 15th and 16th centuries and was endowed by the Guild of Archers.

Guild statue on the Place du Petit-Sablon

Across Rue de la Régence is the smaller **Place du Petit-Sablon**, occupied by a restful ornamental garden containing a sculpture group of the 16th-century Counts Egmont and Hornes, who were executed by the Spanish, and a fountain. The garden is surrounded by 48 columns supporting bronze figurines that represent medieval guilds.

Continuing north along Rue de la Régence, you come to the **Musées Royeaux des Beaux-Arts** (Royal Fine Arts Museums; admission fee), two museums under one roof. First is the **Musée d'Art Ancien** (Museum of Historical Art; open Tues–Sun 10am–noon and 1–5pm), which has paintings by Brueghel the Elder and Brueghel the Younger, Rubens, Van Gogh, Gauguin, Renoir, Jordaens, Ensor, Seurat, Rops and more. Appropriately, you go underground to the **Musée d'Art Moderne** (Museum of Modern Art; open Tues–Sun 10am–1pm and 2–5pm), to view works by the Belgian surrealist René Magritte (1898–1967), whose art played subtle tricks with 'reality', and by Dalí, Permeke, Dufy, Delvaux and others.

Place Royale, a graceful cobblestoned square at the intersection of Rue de la Régence and Rue Royale, has at its centre an equestrian **statue of Duke Godefroy de Bouillon**, who led the First Crusade to the conquest of Jerusalem in 1099, was

Eglise St-Jacques-sur-Coudenburg

appointed Defender of the Holy Sepulchre, and died there in 1100. Behind the statue rise the columns of the 18th-century, neoclassical **Eglise St-Jacques-sur-Coudenberg** (Church of St James on the Coudenberg). Around the square are handsome palazzo-style mansions from the same century.

You go downhill on Rue Montagne de la Cour to the wrought-iron tracery and glass of the former Old England department store, an art nouveau gem from 1899 by Paul Saintenoy that has been restored and now houses the noteworthy collection of the **Musée des Instruments de Musique** (Musical Instruments Museum; open Tues–Fri 9.30am–5pm, Sat–Sun 10am–5pm; admission fee). Further downhill, is the red-brick towered **Hôtel Ravenstein**, a surviving remnant of the 15th-century, late-Gothic Coudenberg Palace of the Low Countries' Burgundian and Habsburg rulers. This reached from here to Place Royale until most of it burned to the ground in 1731. Across the street, stairways lead down to the **Mont des Arts**, an ornamental garden with an equestrian statue of King Albert I at its far end.

Back where Place Royale joins Rue Royale, the **Palais des Beaux-Arts** (Palace of Fine Arts, 'Bozar'), home of the Belgian National Orchestra, has a museum section for temporary exhibits, often of modern art. Across the street, Place des Palais fronts the gardens and façade of the **Palais Royal** (Royal Palace; open for guided tours 21 July–mid-Sept:

Tues–Sun; free), built in phases from 1815 onwards. King Albert's office is here. A Belgian flag flies when the king is in the country, but the royal family's residence is the Palace of Laeken in the northern suburbs. At the side of the palace, the **Musée BELvue** (Museum of the Dynasty; open June–Sept: Tues–Sun 10am–6pm; Oct–May: 10am–5pm; admission fee), in the graceful 18th-century Hôtel de Belle-vue, recounts the history of Belgium.

The king has a splendid view of the **Parc de Bruxelles** (Brussels Park), a former royal hunting reserve that was landscaped into a tree-shaded, French-style park, its avenues and fountains laid out in the shape of Masonic symbols. Beyond the park's far end, Belgium's Parliament meets in the **Palais de la Nation** (National Palace).

The Palais Royal from the Parc de Bruxelles

Continuing along Rue Royale, the **Colonne du Congrès** (Congress Column) commemorates Belgium's 1830 Independence Revolution. Atop its 47-m (153-ft) high shaft stands a statue of King Leopold I. At its base is the Tomb of the Unknown Soldier. Beyond are the glasshouses, rotunda and gardens of the **Jardin Botanique** (Botanical Garden), dating from 1826. It now houses a cultural centre of the French-speaking Community.

The Upper Town

The house at Rue Américaine 25 in Ixelles, where art nouveau architect Victor Horta lived between 1901 and 1919, is
now the **Musée Horta** (Horta Museum; open Tues–Sun
2–5.30pm; admission fee), a testimonial to the flowing lines,
natural shapes and use of light and colour that he employed.

Near the end of busy Avenue Louise, the former Cistercian **Abbaye de la Cambre** is a tranquil abbey, surrounded
by an ornamental garden featuring fountains and pools and
containing the 13th-century church of **Notre-Dame de la
Cambre**. The abbey buildings house an art school and the
National Geographical Institute. Beyond the abbey begins
the city's largest park, the **Bois de la Cambre**. The park
merges with the **Forêt de Soignes**, the remnant of an an-

Art Nouveau

For all the demolition of architectural gems in recent decades, the tide
seems to be turning towards preserving what remains of a remarkable heritage. And despite being the capital of so many other things,
Brussels is perhaps proudest of being the 'capital of art nouveau',
having been bequeathed some of the finest architecture of this exu-
berant turn-of-the-20th-century style. Property 'developers' and local
government connivance have conspired to destroy some buildings,
but others remain to dazzle the eye.

The foremost proponent of art nouveau was Brussels architect
Victor Horta *(see above)*, some of whose students continued the tradition. Notable examples of the genre are the Solvay Mansion, the
cafés De Ultieme Hallucinatie and Le Falstaff, the Maisons Waucquez
department store (which houses the Belgian Comic Strip Centre), the
Old England department store (which houses the Museum of Musical
Instruments), the Tassel House, the florist De Backer, and townhouses
in Square Ambiorix and Square Marie-Louise.

cient forest that stretches beyond the city's suburbs. Walking, cycling and horse-riding paths course among the trees. Autumn is especially beautiful.

Les Marolles

The brooding presence of the Palais de Justice looms over this low-income district. In addition, the Marolles is under siege by gentrifiers from the neighbouring, wealthy Sablon district. Despite all this, the

Shoppers in the Marolles

Marolliens have retained their community spirit, obscure dialect and iconoclastic view of life. Brussels' finest street market, the **Vieux Marché** (Old Market; daily 7am–2pm), takes place here, in Place du Jeu de Balle. People flock to this flea-market for bargains.

The Cinquantenaire

Designed to celebrate 50 years of Belgian independence in 1880 – though elements of it missed this deadline by decades – the Cinquantenaire complex, east of the city centre, is an assertion of national pride. At the heart of the **Parc du Cinquantenaire** (Golden Jubilee Park) is the triumphal Arc du Cinquantenaire (Golden Jubilee Arch), a symbol of the nation's unity, surmounted by a four-horse chariot.

Amid all this patriotic posturing, the **Musée du Cinquantenaire** (Cinquantenaire Museum; open Tues–Fri 9.30am–5pm; Sat–Sun 10am–5pm; admission fee) provides a feast of ancient art and artefacts. Among the exhibits is a superb

In the Musée du Cinquantenaire

model of imperial Rome. Patriotism pops up again next door in the **Musée Royal de l'Armée et d'Histoire Militaire** (Royal Museum of the Army and Military History; open Tues–Sun 9am–noon and 1–4.45pm; free), which has a large, fascinating display of weaponry, uniforms and military equipment.

Vehicles are on display at the Cinquantenaire's third museum, **Autoworld** (open Apr–Sept: daily 10am–6pm; Oct–Mar: Mon–Fri 10am–5pm, Sat–Sun 10am–6pm; admission fee). Among the many vintage and classic cars exhibited here are Belgian Minervas and Imperias.

Around the Periphery

Begun in 1905 and completed in 1970, the massive **Basilique Nationale du Sacré-Coeur** (National Basilica of the Sacred Heart), in Koekelberg in the northwest, looks something like a modern take on a Byzantine basilica. A gallery in the prominent dome affords a panoramic view of Brussels.

Anderlecht, in the southwest, features the **Maison Erasme** (Erasmus House; open Tues–Sun 10am–5pm; admission fee), a memorial to the humanist philosopher Erasmus in the house in Rue du Chapitre where he lived in 1521. Not far away, in Rue Gheude, the **Musée de la Gueuze** (Gueuze Museum; open Mon–Fri 9am–5pm, Sat 10am–5pm; admission fee), in a family-owned brewery, celebrates traditional Brussels beers.

The Royal Estate and Environs

Just north of Brussels, in **Laeken**, is the palace where the royal family lives. Some insight into their lives can be gained on a visit to the palace's 19th-century, wrought-iron-and-glass **Serres Royales** (Royal Greenhouses; open for guided tours Apr–May, variable dates; free), where trees, plants and flowers from around the world are installed in a regal setting.

On the edge of the estate, two exotic structures mirror the eclectic tastes of Belgium's architect-king, Leopold II: the **Pavillon Chinois** (Chinese Pavilion) and the **Tour Japonais** (Japanese Tower; both open Tues–Sun 10am–4.45pm; admission fee). The former, a faithful imitation of a Chinese temple, from 1909, contains antique Chinese and Japanese porcelain; the latter, a red-painted imitation Zen-Buddhist pagoda, from 1904, houses Oriental artefacts. Both were built with authentic imported materials and the aid of native craftsmen.

The Pavillon Chinois at Laeken

Mini-Europe, with the Atomium in the background

Bruparck and Environs

To the north of Laeken is the ever-popular **Atomium** (reopens spring 2006; usually open daily 10am–6pm; admission fee), an instantly recognisable symbol of Brussels. Built for the 1958 World's Fair, it stands 105m (345ft) tall and its nine huge connected metal spheres represent an iron atom enlarged 165 million times. You get a fine view from the upper-sphere observation deck.

Bruparck is a modern attractions-and-entertainment zone. Pride of place belongs to **Mini-Europe** (open mid-Mar–June, Sept: 9.30am–6pm; July–Aug: 9.30am–8pm; Oct–Jan: 10am–6pm; 'Mini-Europe by Night', late July–late Aug: 9.30am–midnight; admission fee), which on a scale of 1:25 reproduces some of the European Union's finest architectural and engineering achievements. You can stroll among the Parthenon, the Palace of Westminster, the Leaning Tower of Pisa, the Arc de Triomphe, the Brandenburg Gate, the Channel Tunnel, the Ariane rocket, and more.

THE BRUSSELS HINTERLAND

The hinterland of Brussels is sufficiently interesting to justify side trips from the capital. The region incorporates the low hills of Dutch-speaking Flemish Brabant and French-speaking Walloon Brabant, two separate provinces created in the 1990s out of the former, single Brabant province.

Tervuren

Just east of Brussels, in **Tervuren**, the **Koninklijke Museum
voor Midden-Afrika/Musée Royal de l'Afrique Centrale**
(Royal Museum of Central Africa; open Tues–Fri 10am–5pm,
Sat–Sun 10am–6pm; admission fee), was created as an expres-
sion of colonial pride in the Belgian Congo (Democratic Re-
public of Congo). Set in a royal estate from 1910, off
Leuvensesteenweg, the museum now takes a more enlightened
approach to tropical ethnography and ecology.

Idyllic **Genval**, southeast of Brussels, has an attractive small
lake, the **Lac de Genval**, surrounded by wealthy villas and fine
cafés and restaurants. Nearby **Louvain-la-Neuve** is a university town, purpose-built to house the Francophone Université
Catholique de Louvain (Catholic University of Louvain),
which moved here in 1970 when the venerable Catholic
University of Leuven splintered along Belgium's language

Sculpture group at the Royal Museum of Central Africa

Butte du Lion, dominating the Waterloo battlefield

fault-line. The campus is interesting for its innovative modern architecture. Despite being in ruins, the 12th-century Cistercian abbey near **Villers-la-Ville** (open Apr–Oct: daily 10am–6pm; Nov–Mar: Wed–Mon 10am–5pm; admission fee), south of the city, evokes the atmosphere of Europe's great medieval religious foundations.

Southwest of the city, at Beersel, you can visit the moated, 14th-century **Kasteel van Beersel** (Beersel Castle; open Mar–mid-Nov: Tues–Sun 10am–noon and 2–6pm; mid-Nov–Dec, and Feb: Sat–Sun; admission fee). A little way north of Brussels, at the village of Meise, the **Nationale Planentuin** (National Botanic Gardens; open daily 9.30am–dusk; admission fee) occupies a large, open estate, the Domein Van Boechout, with a restored 13th-century castle at its heart, a lake and a wide variety of trees, plants and flowers. The most exotic specimens are in the greenhouses of the **Plantenpaleis** (Plant Palace).

➤ Waterloo

The decisive Battle of Waterloo on 18 June, 1815 was fought on farmland south of Brussels, around the hamlets of Mont-St-Jean and Plancenoit. Access to the most important battlefield sites is via the **Centre du Visiteur** (Visitor Centre; open Apr–Oct: daily 9.30am–6.30pm; Nov–Mar: daily 10am–5pm; admission fee, and combined admission fee for other attractions), where film and graphic presentations illustrate the battle's epic scale and the tactics employed.

From here, you can climb the 226 steps of the **Butte du Lion** (Lion Mound), a 40-m (130-ft) high artificial hill that was created in 1826 on the spot where Holland's Prince William of Orange was wounded. The mound, which affords a commanding view over the battlefield, is topped by a cast-iron lion on a plinth. More aid to the imagination is provided in the **Panorama**, where a dramatic diorama painting illustrates the furious but fruitless French cavalry charge led by Marshal Ney. The nearby **Musée des Cires** (Waxworks Museum) includes wax images of Napoleon, Wellington and Blücher. In Waterloo, which has grown to a small town, the **Musée Wellington** (Wellington Museum; open Apr–Sept: daily 9.30am–6.30pm; Oct–Mar: daily 10.30am–5pm; admission fee) has more memorabilia in an inn that was Wellington's headquarters.

Battle of Waterloo

One of many surprising aspects of the Battle of Waterloo is that it did not take place at Waterloo at all, but in rolling fields 4km (2.5 miles) further south where the road from Brussels, after passing through the Forêt de Soignes and Waterloo, arrives at a low ridge beyond the farm of Mont-St-Jean. A traveller taking this route on 18 June, 1815, would here have run into French Emperor Napoleon Bonaparte and his 75,000 troops, doing their headlong best to go in the opposite direction.

More surprising by far, is that Napoleon, who won an empire through his supreme grasp of the military art, lost it in the end by putting his head down and charging repeatedly uphill in vain and bloody attempts to shift the Duke of Wellington's 72,000-man army blocking the road to Brussels. 'If my orders are properly executed,' Napoleon told his generals before kicking off the carnage, 'we will sleep tonight in Brussels.' The superb courage of the French soldiers came near to confirming their emperor's prediction. Wellington called the contest 'the nearest run thing you ever saw in your life'.

Leuven

This historic town, 15km (9 miles) east of Brussels, is the capital of Vlaams-Brabant (Flemish Brabant). Its highly regarded **Katholiek Universiteit Leuven** (Catholic University of Leuven), one of Europe's oldest universities, dates from 1425. Erasmus taught here between 1516 and 1521. The cafés in the gabled former merchants' houses that line the cobblestoned **Oude Markt** are favoured haunts of the town's large and boisterous student community.

More sober – though flamboyant in its own way – is the 15th-century **Stadhuis** (Town Hall) in the Grote Markt, a lavish late-Gothic tracery of intricately carved façades, spires and sculptures that is arguably the most beautiful in the Low Countries. Students now bunk in the small, red-brick 13th-century houses set around the courtyard of the **Groot Begijnhof** (Large Beguinage) in Schapenstraat, which formerly housed religious women.

Leuven Stadhuis (Town Hall)

Mechelen

Midway between Antwerp and Brussels, Mechelen, the seat of Belgium's Catholic Church and a centre of carillon music, experienced a moment of glory during the 16th century, when it was the Habsburg local capital.

For all of its 97m (318ft), the belfry of **Sint Rombouts-**

kathedraal (St Rombold's Cathedral; open Apr–Sept: Mon–Sat 7.30am–7.30pm, Sun 2–7pm; Oct–Mar: Mon–Sat 7.30am–4pm, Sun 2–4pm; free) in the Grote Markt, is shorter than was planned. Still, the tower, begun in the 13th century and completed in the 16th, dominates the town and contains

> Mechelen is the home of the Koninklijke Beiaardschool (Royal Carillon School), where musicians from around the world are trained to play the bells of carillons like the one in the belfry of St Rombold's Cathedral.

two 49-bell carillons. Among the cathedral's works of art is Van Dyck's *Christ on the Cross Between Two Criminals*.

The neighbouring **Stadhuis** (Town Hall) is in two parts: the 14th-century Gothic **Lakenhalle** (Cloth Hall) and the 16th-century Flemish Renaissance **Paleis van de Grote Raad** (Palace of the Grand Council).

Mechelen's premier museum, the **Museum Hof van Busleyden** (open Tues–Sun 10am–5pm; admission fee), in a mansion dating from 1503 in Merodestraat, north of the Grote Markt, contains paintings, tapestries, sculptures, furnishings and other items from medieval to modern times. In the associated **Beiaardmuseum** (Carillon Museum) are carillon bells, keyboards and associated items.

ANTWERP

The city of Rubens, Antwerp (Antwerpen) is Europe's second biggest port. Ships once moored at wharves along the Scheldt in the centre of Antwerp to load and unload their cargoes. The harbour has shifted to a vast complex of docks downstream. More than 16,000 ships tie up annually, delivering and collecting more than 100 million tonnes of cargo. The city is also a centre of the international diamond trade, and has an animated cultural and nightlife scene.

Antwerp is the world's centre for trade in diamonds. Most of the cutting, polishing and trading takes place in the Diamond Quarter, where the offices of the Hoge Raad voor Diamant (Diamond High Council) and the Beurs voor Diamanthandel (Diamond Exchange) stand amid a glittering array of jewellery shops.

The architecture of its **Centraal Station** in Koningin Astridplein seems more like that of a domed marble temple than a railway station. Beside the station, the **Dierentuin** (Zoo; open daily May–June and Sept: 10am–6pm; July–Aug: until 7pm; Mar–Apr and Oct: until 5.30 pm; Nov–Feb: until 4.45pm; admission fee) is known for its conservation work with threatened species.

Diamond Quarter

Also in the Centraal Station neighbourhood is the **Diamantkwartier** (Diamond Quarter), the centre of the city's diamond trade. On Koningin Astridplein, the **Diamantmuseum Provincie Antwerpen** (Province of Antwerp Diamond Museum; open Thur–Tues 10am–5.30pm) includes a reproduction of the South African Cullinan diamond, the largest ever found.

At the heart of Antwerp, the **Grote Markt's** handsome 16th-century Flemish guildhalls are outshone by the Renaissance **Stadhuis** (Town Hall; open for guided tours Mon–Thur at 2pm; admission fee). A fountain-sculpture in the middle of the square depicts a legend of the city's name: a Roman soldier, Silvius Brabo, throws away the severed hand of the giant Antigonus, who had threatened ships on the River Scheldt – in Dutch this would be *handwerpen*: 'throwing a hand'.

Cathedral and Castle

➤ The magnificent **Onze-Lieve-Vrouwekathedraal** (Cathedral of Our Lady; open Mon–Fri 10am–5.30pm, Sat 10am–3pm,

Sun 10am–4pm; admission fee), behind the Grote Markt in Handschoenmarkt, was begun in 1352. Its interior suffered at the hands of Protestant rioters during the Iconoclastic Fury of 1566, but is enhanced by three Rubens paintings: *The Raising of the Cross*, *The Descent from the Cross*, and *The Resurrection*. The 123-m (403-ft) high spire, the highest in the Low Countries, soars above the city's skyline. Across from the cathedral, with an entrance at Oude Koornmarkt 16, **Vlaeykensgang** is a tranquil medieval courtyard.

The gloomy **Steen** (Castle; open Tues–Sun 10am–4.45pm; admission fee) stands on the Scheldt west of the Grote Markt. This turreted 16th-century fortification is home to the model ships, paintings and nautical paraphernalia of the **Nationaal Scheepvaartmuseum** (National Maritime Museum), which spreads out onto the adjacent wharves, where real ships are moored. From a quay on the Scheldt adjacent to the Steen, the Flandria company operates boat tours along the river and to Antwerp harbour, as well as cruises to more distant points, such as Ghent, Bruges and Oostende.

Rubens had a hand in the design and adornment of the early 17th-century **Sint-Carolus Borromeuskerk** (St Charles Borromeo Church; open Mon–Fri 10am–

Antwerp Cathedral, with a statue of Rubens

Inside Antwerp's church of St Charles Borromeo

12.30pm and 2–5pm, Sat 10am–6pm; admission fee) in Hendrik Conscienceplein, east of the Grote Markt. Like many of Antwerp's wealthy patricians of the time, Rubens, who died in 1640, is buried in **Sint-Jacobskerk** (St James's Church; open Apr–Oct: daily 2–5pm; Nov–Mar: Mon–Sat 9am–noon; admission fee), a 15th-century Gothic foundation overlayed with 17th-century baroque, further to the east in Lange Nieuwstraat. The artist's vault is in a chapel behind the altar.

To the north in Rodestraat, Antwerp's 16th-century **Begijnhof** (Beguinage), formerly a religious institution for lay-women, is today a tranquil cluster of small houses.

South of the centre, at No. 9 Wapper, a house from 1610 is the **Rubenshuis** (Rubens House; open Tues–Sun 10am–4.45pm; admission fee), where Peter Paul Rubens lived and painted. The house, the artist's workshop and the courtyard garden have been restored to evoke the time of Rubens. The

Plantin-Moretus Museum (open Tues–Sun 10am–5pm; admission fee) displays rare antique books in a building in Vrijdagmarkt where the printer Christopher Plantin founded a printing shop in 1548.

Following the international success of the 'Antwerp Six' fashion designers, the city has opened a striking fashion museum, **MoMu** (open Tues–Sun 10am–6pm, admission fee), in a former 19th-century hotel.

South of the Steen, and known as MUHKA, the **Museum voor Hedendaagse Kunst Antwerpen** (Antwerp Museum of Modern Art; open Tues–Sun 10am–5pm; admission fee) occupies a former warehouse, part of Antwerp's old port facilities, in Leuvenstraat, close to the Scheldt. Behind the warehouse's original art deco façade, a collection of cutting-edge Belgian and international art fills the enormous interior.

Fine Arts Museum

South of the city centre in Leopold de Waelplaats is the city's top art museum, the **Koninklijke Museum voor Schone Kunsten Antwerpen** (Antwerp Royal Fine Arts Museum; open Tues–Sat 10am–5pm, Sun 10am–6pm; admission fee). In a neoclassical building dating from 1890, the gallery has an extensive collection of works by Flemish Masters, among them Jan van Eyck, Rogier van der Weyden, the German-born Hans Memling, Rubens, Jacob Jordaens and Antoon Van Dyck, and Pieter Brueghel

Education of the Virgin by Peter Paul Rubens, in the Antwerp Royal Fine Arts Museum

the Elder and the Younger. There are also works by modern Belgians, including James Ensor, René Magritte and Paul Delvaux.

Around Antwerp

Lier, a small town on the River Nete 16km (10 miles) southeast of Antwerp, has a remarkable tower, the **Zimmertoren** (Zimmer Tower; open Apr–Sept: daily, 9am–noon and 1.30–6pm; Oct–Mar: daily 9am–noon and 1.30–5.30pm; admission fee), situated in the Zimmerplein, the town's central square. In 1930, local astronomy enthusiast Lodewijk Zimmer fitted out the exterior of the 14th-century tower with the **Jubelklok** (Centenary Clock), which incorporates representations of astronomical objects and calculations. Inside is the **Wonderklok** (Wonder Clock) and other astronomical mechanisms.

Lier Stadhuis (Town Hall)

Sint-Niklaas, 20km (12.5 miles) southwest of Antwerp, has the largest **Grote Markt** in Belgium, embellished by a 19th-century neo-Gothic **Stadhuis** (Town Hall).

At Kalmthout, north of Antwerp near the Dutch border, are the sand dunes, heath and forest of the **Natuurreservaat De Kalmthoutse Heide** (Kalmthout Heath Nature Reserve), and the thousands of variegated trees and plants of **Arboretum Kalmthout** (open daily 10am–5pm; admission fee).

THE KEMPEN

A broad expanse of heathland east of Antwerp along the Dutch border, the Kempen is traversed by streams and canals, and dotted with lakes. Once isolated and difficult to access, it is popular with tourists for its nature reserves, tranquil villages and abbeys.

Turnhout

The northernmost town likely thinks of itself as lucky – making playing cards is a big deal here. This is reflected at the **Nationaal Museum van de Speelkaart** (National Playing Card Museum; open Tues–Sat 2–5pm, Sun 11am–5pm; admission fee) in Druivenstraat near the Grote Markt, in a factory where cards were once produced.

Archaeological finds from prehistoric, Celtic, Roman and Frankish times, and folklore items, are displayed at the nearby **Taxandria Museum** (open Tues–Sat 2–5pm, Sun 11am–5pm; admission fee) in Begijnenstraat. The museum name comes from the Roman name for the Kempen.

South of Turnhout, near Geel, is **Bobbejaanland** (open early Apr–late Oct from 10am; see <www.bobbejaanland.be> for daily schedule; admission fee), a country-and-western-themed adventure park with a cowboy-style show.

An old fortified town between Turnhout and Geel, **Diest** contains much of historical interest. The 14th–16th-century

Sint-Sulpitiuskerk (Church of St Sulpice; open mid-May–June and first two weeks Sept: Sun 2–5pm; July–Aug: daily 2–5pm; church free, admission fee for treasury) in the Grote Markt, is rich in religious art and has a superb baroque organ. The cellars of the 18th-century **Stadhuis** (Town Hall), in the Grote Markt, the **Stedelijk Museum** (Municipal Museum; open Mar–Sept: daily 10am–noon and 1–5pm; Oct–Feb: Mon–Sat; admission fee) contain a small but interesting medieval collection.

Hasselt

The town is a potent name in Belgium as a centre of the *jenever* (gin) industry and home of the **Nationaal Jenevermuseum** (National Gin Museum; open Apr–Oct: Tues–Sun 10am–5pm; Nov–Mar: Tues–Fri 10am–5pm, Sat–Sun 1–5pm; admission fee) in Witte Nonnenstraat. A stroll here amid distilling gear and bottles ends with a taste of the best-loved creations.

➤   The **Provinciaal Domein Bokrijk** (open Apr–Sept: daily 10am–6pm; Oct–Mar: Mon–Fri 9am–4pm; admission fee), northeast of Hasselt, has an **Openluchtmuseum** (Open-Air Museum), dedicated to the historic way of life in Flanders. Old crafts are presented in farms, windmills and cottages by people wearing traditional costume, and there are demonstrations of traditional sports.

Tongeren

Somewhere near Belgium's oldest town, tribes led by Ambiorix won a victory over Julius Caesar's Roman legions in 54BC. The Gallic chieftain is honoured with a statue in Tongeren's Grote Markt. Also in the Grote Markt, the 13th- to 15th-century **Onze-Lieve-Vrouwebasiliek** (Basilica of Our Lady; open daily 9am–4pm; treasury Apr–Sept; basilica free, admission fee to treasury) is richly ornamented. Among the items in its **Schatkamer** (Treasury) is a 13th-century reliquary, the *Shrine of the Martyrs of Trier*. Behind the basilica, in Kielenstraat, the **Gallo-Romeinsmuseum** (Gallo-Roman Museum; open Mon noon–5pm, Tues–Fri 9am–5pm, Sat–Sun 10am–6pm; admission fee) houses archaeological finds from the time of Ambiorix and Caesar.

GHENT (GENT)

Ghent is every bit as historic but not as handsome as Bruges, and, not frozen in time, it feels like a real place rather than a museum exhibit. The centre contains many reminders of the medieval mercantile and weaving economy that once made this the most wealthy and populous town north of the Alps.

The heart of Ghent's medieval harbour, the **Korenlei** and **Graslei** quays, facing each other across the River Leie below Sint-Michielsbrug (St Michael's Bridge), are lined with gabled guildhalls in several styles. Boat tours of the city

View of Ghent from Sint Michielsbrug

depart from here. On the far side of Sint-Michielsbrug, the medieval **Sint-Michielskerk** (St Michael's Church) contains religious paintings and sculptures, including *Christ Dying on the Cross* by Antoon van Dyck. Adjacent to Graslei, in Koren-markt, the 13th-century Flemish-Gothic **Sint-Niklaaskerk** (St Nicholas' Church) has an exterior of grey stone.

City of Towers

Ghent is a city of towers and the highest belongs to the 13th-to 14th-century **Belfort en Lakenhalle** (Belfry and Cloth Hall; open mid-Mar–mid-Nov daily 10am–12.30pm and 2–6pm; free guided tours Easter and May–Sept: daily 2.10, 3.10 and 4.10pm; admission fee), a complex of monumental Gothic buildings in Sint-Baafsplein. The 95-m (312-ft) high Belfry affords a superb view over the city, and its carillon is

Flemish Masters

A group of early Flemish artists, based mostly in Bruges and Ghent, have had their work handed down to us under the banner of the 'Flemish Primitives'. Yet the luminous, revolutionary work of Jan van Eyck (1385–1441), whose *Adoration of the Mystic Lamb* is in Ghent's St Bavo's Cathedral, can scarcely be thought of as primitive. Nor can that of his contemporaries Rogier van der Weyden (*circa* 1399–1464), Hans Memling (*circa* 1430–94) and Petrus Christus (*circa* 1410–1472), who shared Van Eyck's fondness for realistic portrayals of human and natural subjects.

Later, the focus of attention switched to Antwerp and, to a lesser degree, to Brussels. The occasionally gruesome works of Pieter Brueghel the Elder (1525–69), the sensuous paintings of Peter Paul Rubens (1577–1640) and the output of Rubens's students Jacob Jordaens (1593–1678) and Antoon van Dyck (1599–1641) cemented the Flemish connection with the finest art of its day.

a symbol of the town's civic pride. The Cloth Hall is testimony to Ghent's medieval heyday, when the cloth trade placed it among Europe's most important cities.

Across the square, the façade of the **Stadhuis** (Town Hall; open for guided tours, May–Oct: Mon–Thur 2.30pm; admission fee) in Botermarkt ranges through architectural periods from late-Gothic to baroque. In-

Jan van Eyck's altarpiece in St Bavo's Cathedral

side, the magnificent **Pacificatiezaal** (Pacification Room), is where the Pacification of Ghent, a treaty aimed (fruitlessly) at ending the religious wars in the Low Countries, was signed in 1576.

Nearby **Sint-Baafskathedraal** (Cathedral of St Bavo; cathedral and crypt open Apr–Oct: Mon–Sat 8.30am–6pm, Sun 1–6pm; Nov–Mar: Mon–Sat 8.30am–5pm, Sun 1–5pm; free; *Mystic Lamb* chapel open Apr–Oct: Mon–Sat 9.30am–5pm, Sun 1–5pm; Nov–Mar: Mon–Sat 10.30am–4pm, Sun 1–4pm; admission fee), a magnificent Gothic construction, is one of Europe's great cathedrals. Its highlight is the *Adoration of the Mystic Lamb* (1432), a triptych altarpiece by Jan van Eyck.

Gravensteen

North of the Leie, at the confluence of the river and the Lieve canal, stands the restored but still gloomy **Gravensteen** (Castle of the Counts; open Apr–Sept: daily 9am–6pm; Oct–Mar: daily 9am–5pm; admission fee), a fortress from 1180 of the counts of Flanders. 'Amenities' behind the squat ramparts include a fully-equipped torture chamber. The castle was later used as a mint, prison and cotton mill. Behind the Gravensteen, **Patershol** district is a jumble of narrow medieval streets, dotted with restaurants and cafés. On waterside Kraanlei, **Het Huis van Alijn** (Alijn House; open Tues–Sun 11am–5pm; admission fee) is Ghent's folklore museum, in the cottages of a centuries-old almshouse. The museum focuses on Ghent around 1900.

West of the Leie, the **Design Museum Gent** (open Tues–Sun 10am–6pm; admission fee) occupies a graceful mansion from 1755 with central courtyard. The rooms display interior design and antique and modern furniture.

Around Ghent

Outside Deurle, 12km (7½ miles) south of Ghent, **Kasteel Ooidonk** (Ooidonk Castle; open Apr–mid-Sept: Sun and hols 2–5.30pm; July–Aug: also Sat 2–5.30pm; admission fee) is a moated 16th-century château with onion-domed towers. **Sint-Martens-Latem**, a scenic village on the River Leie 10km (6 miles) southwest of Ghent, is known as a 'village of artists'. Several modern Flemish painters, among them Gustave de Smet and Constant Permeke, lived and worked here.

This bear at the Burgher's Lodge is a badge of Bruges

BRUGES (BRUGGE)

A beautifully, if almost too perfectly preserved medieval town, Bruges has the air of an outdoor museum and a historic core that's invariably swamped with visitors from around the world. This popularity is fully merited, and a visit is sure to be a highlight of a trip to Belgium.

View from Rozenhoedkaai, the Belfry in the background

The Markt and the Burg

Bruges' main square, the **Markt**, is ranged around with historic guildhalls, most of them converted to restaurants and cafés. In the middle stands a sculpture-group of two 14th-century Flemish heroes of the wars against France, Pieter de Coninck and Jan Breidel. At the south end, the 13th-century **Hallen** (Market Halls) were for centuries the trading heart of Bruges. From them rises the **Belfort** (Belfry; open Tues–Sun 9.30am–5pm, also Easter Mon, Pentecost Mon; admission fee). 84m (275ft) high This dates mostly from the same period as the Hallen but its upper level is 15th century. Inside, 366 steps curve around a steep stairwell to a 47-bell carillon. The adjacent 19th-century neo-Gothic **Provinciaal Hof** (Provincial Palace) is the seat of the West Flanders provincial government.

Impressive though it is, the Markt is neither the town's most handsome nor most historic square. Those distinctions belong to the neighbouring **Burg**, at the end of short Breidelstraat.

Making lace in Bruges

Surrounded by monumental buildings, this cobblestoned square has been the heart of Bruges' civic and religious life since its foundation. The neoclassical **Landhuis van het Brugse Vrije** (Palace of the Liberty of Bruges) houses local government offices and the tourist office. Inside, the **Renaissancezaal Brugse Vrije** (Renaissance Hall of the Liberty of Bruges; open Tues–Sun 9.30am–12.30pm and 1.30–5pm, also Easter Mon, Pentecost Mon; admission fee), has a fine chimneypiece from 1531 in black Dinant marble and oak, depicting the Habsburg Emperor Charles V.

The 14th-century Gothic **Stadhuis** (Town Hall; open Tues–Sun 9.30am–5pm, also Easter Mon, Pentecost Mon; admission fee) was the model for many other such buildings in the Low Countries, and contains the magnificent **Gotische Zaal** (Gothic Hall). Next door, the 16th-century Flemish Renaissance **Oude Civiele Griffie** (Old Recorder's House) has been restored.

On the other side of Blinde-Ezelstraat, the gloomy 14th-century Romanesque **Basiliek van het Heilig Bloed** (Basilica of the Holy Blood; open Apr–Sept: daily 9.30am–noon and 2–6pm; Oct–Mar: Thur–Tues 10am–noon and 2–4pm, Wed 10am– noon; admission fee) contains a venerated relic of the blood of Christ, said to have been brought to Bruges from Jerusalem in 1149 by the crusader Dirk van de Elzas. The blood-stained scrap of cloth, in a rock-crystal phial, is carried in procession on Ascension Day. On the square's northern face, the 17th-century baroque **Proosdij** (Deanery) used to be the palace of the Bishop of Bruges.

Waterfront Attractions

Across the Groene Rei canal, past the covered **Vismarkt** (Fish Market) from 1821, and bustling **Huidenvettersplein**, canalside **Rozenhoedkaai** affords a lovely view of the Belfry and the central waterfront houses and bridges.

Along Dijver, a tree-fringed canalside south of the Burg, and venue of the weekend antiques market, the **Groeninge Museum** (open Tues–Sun 9.30am–5pm, also Easter Mon, Pentecost Mon; admission fee) holds important works by the 'Flemish Primitives', painters who include Jan van Eyck and Hans Memling *(see box on page 50)*. Van Eyck is represented by his *Madonna with Canon George van der Paele*. Also outstanding is *The Last Judgement* by Hieronymus Bosch.

A restored tracery of rose-coloured stone, the neighbouring 15th-century mansion of the Gruuthuse family is now the **Gruuthuse Museum** (open Tues–Sun 9.30am–5pm, also Easter Mon, Pentecost Mon; admission fee). The collection includes musical instruments, silks, tapestries, furniture and artwork.

Across a small bridge is the **Onze-Lieve-Vrouwekerk** (open Tues–Fri 9.30am–12.30pm and 1.30–5pm, Sat 9.30am–12.30pm and 1.30–4pm, Sun 1.30–5pm). The 13th-century church is topped with a 122-m (400-ft)

A tour (Mar–Nov: 10am–6pm; tour fee) through the Bruges canals in an open boat is delightful, and the view from the water is memorable. Boats depart from several landing stages around the centre and all cover the same route.

high spire, and highlights of the interior are the magnificent tombs of Charles the Bold and Mary and an exquisite *Madonna and Child* sculpture, in Carrara marble, by Michelangelo.

Outside in Mariastraat is a fine example of Bruges Gothic, the 15th-century **Sint-Janshospitaal** (St John's Hospital). Among other uses, it houses the **Memling Museum** (open Tues–Sun 9.30am–5pm, also Easter Mon, Pentecost Mon; admission fee), filled with works by the German-born Flemish Primitive painter Hans Memling.

Reached by bridge across the canal, the **Begijnhof** (Beguinage) is a circle of whitewashed cottages and a church that form a courtyard around a tree-shaded lawn. It was founded in 1245 as a community for *begijns*, religious lay-women whose vows and rule were less strict than those of nuns, but most of the buildings date from 16th century. There are no longer any *begijns*; the Begijnhof is now a Benedictine convent.

In Peperstraat, east of the central canal, is the **Kantcentrum** (Lace Centre; open Mon–Fri 10am–noon and 2–6pm, Sat 10am–noon and 2–5pm; admission fee), a museum and workshop in the 15th-century Jeruzalemgodshuizen (Jerusalem Almshouses), featuring fine displays of lace-making and demonstrations of the craft.

Tapestry-making, a flourishing craft from the 15th to the 18th century, employing 50,000 weavers in Flanders at its height, has almost disappeared. Fine surviving tapestries – including some containing gold and silver thread – can be seen in town halls and museums across the land.

Damme

Damme is an attractive canalside village 7km (4 miles) east of Bruges. You can get there aboard a small paddle-steamer, the *Lamme Goedzak*. The village is noted for its 15th-century **Stadhuis** (Town Hall), second-hand bookshops and cluster of traditional restaurants.

The beach at De Haan

BEACHES AND CEMETERIES

Despite considerable development, Belgium's 70km (44 miles) of North Sea coastline still has some quiet beaches between the main resorts, and protected nature reserves. Within easy reach of the coast is the city of Ypres and the surrounding war cemeteries of the Flanders Fields.

Ostend (Oostende)

Midway along the coast, Ostend is the largest and busiest resort and has a harbour for fishing boats and freight vessels. Its reputation as a seafood centre is based in part on a cluster of restaurants along harbourside Visserskaai. In the 19th-century, Ostend was among Europe's classiest resorts.

The Anglo-Belgian artist James Ensor (1860–1949), a precursor to Expressionism, was born in Ostend and lived here for most of his life. The **James Ensorhuis** (James Ensor House; open June–Sept: Wed–Mon 10am–noon and

2–5pm; Nov–May: Sat–Sun 2–5pm; admission fee), at Vlaanderenstraat 27, his home from 1916 until his death, contains his studio and has been preserved as a museum of his life and work.

In the harbour floats the distinctive shape of the white-painted, three-masted sailing ship *Mercator* (open Apr–June and Sept: daily 10am–1pm and 2–6pm; July–Aug: daily 10am–7pm; Oct–Mar: Sat–Sun and public holidays 11am–1pm and 2–5pm; admission fee), formerly a merchant marine training ship and now a maritime museum.

Hôtel des Brasseurs, a *belle-époque* building in De Haan

North of Ostend

A medley of restored *belle-époque* villas delights the eye at **De Haan**, 12 km (7½ miles) from Ostend, an elegant small resort that has not permitted the building of high-rise apartment blocks.

The main attractions of **Blankenberge**, aside from its beach, are the seafront **Kursaal-Casino** and the yacht-filled harbour with a lighthouse. Although not especially attractive as a resort, **Zeebrugge** is Belgium's main North Sea port.

There are fine beaches at **Knokke-Heist**, as well as upmarket shopping and residential districts. **Natuur-reservaat Het Zwin** (Zwin Nature Reserve; open Easter–Sept: daily 9am–7pm; Oct–Easter: Thur–Tues 9am–5pm; admission fee), between Knokke-Heist and the Dutch border, is a haven for migrating and breeding birds, including avocets, snipes, storks, plovers, geese and ducks. It was an inlet of the North Sea until it silted up to create the pre-

A great way to tour Belgium's 70-km (44-mile) North Sea coastline is aboard the Kusttram (Coast Tram), which makes a two-hour journey covering all important points, and many minor ones, between De Panne and Knokke-Heist.

sent tidal wetland. The reserve covers an area of 150 hectares (370 acres).

South of Ostend

Belgium's premier fishing port, **Nieuwpoort**, has a reputa-tion for seafood and there is a long line of fishmongers flanking the harbour. An equestrian statue of the World War I 'Soldier King' Albert I stands where the River Ijzer enters the harbour.

Oostduinkerke is notable for its remarkable **Paardevissers** (Horseback Fishermen), who catch shrimps just off the beach, wearing yellow oilskins and using sturdy horses to work the waves. Blustery winds and firm sand have made **De Panne** ideal for the exhilarating sport of sand-yachting. Some 340 hectares (840 acres) of sand dunes form the **Natuurreservaat De Westhoek** (Westhoek Nature Reserve; open permanently; free), between De Panne and the French border.

Just 6km (4 miles) behind the coast, **Veurne** was a Span-ish garrison town during the Habsburg Empire. The town's 17th-century **Grote Markt** is a harmonious Flemish Renais-sance ensemble, typified by the **Stadhuis** (Town Hall; open Apr–Oct: Mon–Sat 11am–2pm and 3–4.30pm; Nov–Mar: Mon–Sat 11am–3pm; admission fee), which has an ornately

Ypres' 13th-century Cloth Hall

embellished loggia. The monumental 13th-century **Sint-Walburgakerk** (St Walburga's Church) is the focus of Veurne's annual Procession of the Penitents.

Ypres

In the Middle Ages, this was among the wealthiest of the Flemish cloth towns. Totally destroyed in World War I (1914–18), when it was the focus of some of the bloodiest battles, Ypres subsequently became a symbol of rebirth after being rebuilt along much the same lines as before.

A colossal token of the town's medieval riches, the magnificent, 13th-century Gothic **Lakenhalle** (Cloth Hall) in the Grote Markt was rebuilt from the ground up after the war. Inside, the **In Flanders Fields Museum** (open Apr–Sept: daily 10am–6pm; Oct–Mar: Tues–Sun 10am–5pm; closed Jan; admission fee) superbly evokes the four years of trench warfare in the Ypres Salient. From the centre of the Cloth Hall rises the **Belfort** (Belfry), 70m (228ft) tall, with 264 interior steps leading to a viewing gallery overlooking the town.

Behind the Cloth Hall is the impressive 13th-century Gothic **Sint-Martenskathedraal** (St Martin's Cathedral; open daily 8am–8pm; free), with a graceful spire. It contains the tomb of a 17th-century Bishop of Ypres, Cornelius Jansenius, whose doctrine of predestination, known as Jansenism, was condemned by the pope as heretical.

Across Elverdingsestraat, the Anglican **St George's Memorial Church**, from 1929, is filled with memorials to the British and Commonwealth soldiers who died in the Ypres Salient.

Another memorial to the fallen, in this case to 54,896 British soldiers killed around Ypres between 1914 and 15 August, 1917, and who have no known grave, is to be found beyond the far side of the Grote Markt. The names are carved on the **Meensepoort** (Menen Gate), the 'Missing Memorial', a white-marble arch that spans a gateway in Ypres' 17th-century walls. Every evening at 8 o'clock, traffic through the gate is suspended for a few minutes while uniformed Ypres firefighters play the *Last Post*.

War Cemeteries

Around Ypres are no fewer than 185 military cemeteries. Perhaps the most beautiful is the **Tyne Cot Commonwealth Military Cemetery**, between Zonnebeke and Passendale (Passchendaele), containing 12,000 graves and a Cross of Remembrance in white Portland stone. The **Deutsche Soldatenfriedhof** (German Soldiers Cemetery)

The Tyne Cot Cemetery

Oudenaarde's Town Hall

at Langemark holds 44,000 dead, some of them members of the Student Regiments killed in the 'Massacre of the Innocents'. There are many monuments to the fallen and you can find concrete pill-boxes and brief stretches of preserved trenches, like the one at **Sanctuary Wood**, complete with shellholes and broken trees.

Kortrijk, Oudenaarde

The market town of **Kortrijk**, close to the French border, has a notable **Begijnhof** (Beguinage) from 1238, just off the Grote Markt. Most of its small white-washed houses with red-tiled roofs are 17th century. Nearby is the Gothic **Sint-Martinuskerk** (St Martin's Church), whose belfry looms above the Begijnhof. Over the border in East Flanders, **Oudenaarde**, a tapestry-making centre in the 15th century, is a gracious town on the Scheldt, with cafés clustered around the atmospheric Grote Markt. Its 16th-century **Stadhuis** (Town Hall; open for guided tours Apr–Oct: Mon–Fri 11am and 3pm; Sat–Sun 2pm and 4pm; admission fee), richly decorated with Flemish Gothic tracery, is adjacent to the 13th-century Gothic **Lakenhalle**.

South of Oudenaarde, the Scheldt undergoes a name change as it flows across Belgium's Dutch-French language frontier, being known as the Escaut in Wallonia (and France) and the Schelde in Flanders.

HAINAUT AND THE SOUTH

The rolling countryside of the southern 'green province' of Hainaut is dotted with farms and cut by canals and the River Scheldt (Escaut). Around Charleroi is an economically troubled area of closed coal-mines and rusting heavy industry, but Hainaut also has the art towns of Mons and Tournai.

Tournai

Tournai, on the Sheldt, is one of Belgium's oldest cities. Following the collapse of Roman power, it was the capital of the Franks. Their King Childeric's burial chamber, which contained a wealth of gold objects (now in Paris), was discovered in 1653. As the seat of a bishop, Tournai was an important ecclesiastical centre in the Middle Ages .

This importance is reflected in the colossal **Cathédrale Notre-Dame** (Cathedral of Our Lady; open Apr–Oct: daily 9.30am–noon and 2–5.30pm; Nov–Mar: daily 10am–noon and 2–4pm; cathedral free, admission fee for treasury), in Place de l'Evêché just off the Grand-Place. The cathedral, which has five towers, is a harmonious Romanesque and Gothic ensemble begun in the 12th century and continued through subsequent centuries. Stained-glass windows suffuse the interior with colour. Among the outstanding works on view in the **Trésor** (Treasury) is the intricate, gold-and-silver **Châsse de Notre-Dame** (Reliquary of our Lady) from 1205. The adjacent 12th-century **Beffroi** (Belfry; open Mar–Oct:

Tournai Cathedral interior

Tues–Sun 10am–1pm and 2–6.30pm; Nov–Feb: Tues–Sun 10am–noon and 2–5pm; admission fee), 72m (236ft) high and holding a 43-bell carillon, affords a superb view of Tournai, which you can experience by climbing the 256 interior steps.

Off the Grand-Place are two interesting museums. The **Musée du Folklore** (Folklore Museum; open Apr–Oct: Wed–Mon 9.30am–12.30pm and 2–5.30pm; Nov–Mar: Wed–Mon 10am–noon and 2–5pm and Sun 10am–noon only; admission fee), in a 17th-century mansion, includes a scale-model of the city as it was in the 16th century. In a mansion from 1825, the **Musée de la Tapisserie** (Tapestry Museum; for opening times see Folklore Museum above; admission fee) has mostly modern tapestries.

Tournai's **Musée des Beaux-Arts** (Museum of Fine Arts; for opening times see Folklore Museum above; admission fee), in Enclos St-Martin, occupies a bright gallery from 1928 designed by architect Victor Horta. Among its collection are paintings by the Tournai-born Flemish Primitive Rogier van der Weyden, and by Rubens and Brueghel.

Between Tournai and Mons, the 17th-century **Château de Beloeil** (Beloeil Castle; open Apr: Sat–Sun 1–6pm; May–Nov: daily 1–6pm; admission fee) has a lavish interior and superb gardens with a lake.

Belgium's rivers and canals, among them the rivers Scheldt and Meuse and the Albert and Central canals, are busy with barge traffic going to and fro between Antwerp, Ghent, Liège, Zeebrugge and other ports. Some barge families still live and work on the water.

Mons

The town's history dates back to the Romans and today Mons is the location of the headquarters of SHAPE (Supreme Headquarters Allied Powers Europe).

At the highest point in the town is the oddly shaped **Bef-**

froi (Belfry) and near it stands the Gothic **Collégiale Ste-Waudru** (Church of St Waudru), from 1450, named after a local saint. Inside is the **Car d'Or** (Golden Coach), which is used in an annual religious procession.

In the **Grand-Place**, the 15th-century **Hôtel de Ville** (Town Hall; visits only by reservation) contains a number of interesting paintings and tapestries.

The area around Mons was the scene of heavy fighting in World War I, and the **Musée d'Histoire Militaire** (Museum of Military History; open Tues–Sat noon–6pm, Sun 10am–noon and 2–6pm, admission fee) has

Detail on the Theatre Royal on Mons' Grand-Place

an impressive collection of military relics from that time. The tourist office has created a signposted route indicating the area's main military cemeteries and monuments.

In the Hornu district is an unusual monument of industrial history. **Grand-Hornu** (open Tues–Sun 10am–6pm; admission fee), a coal mine from 1825, was an effort to create a utopian working and living environment. The works are now in ruins but the houses have been restored. On the southern edge of Mons, in Cuesmes, the restored **Maison Van Gogh** (Van Gogh House; open Tues–Sun 10am–6pm; admission fee), at No. 3 Rue du Pavillon, is where the Dutch artist lived and worked as a lay missionary in 1878–9.

East of Mons, at La Louvière, from May to September you can board a canal boat for a tour on the **Canal Historique du Centre** (Historic Central Canal), which includes being taken up on hydraulic boat-lifts that are a UNESCO World Heritage Site. More canal-boat trips are on offer north of La Louvière, at the **Plan Incliné de Ronquières** (Inclined Plane of Ronquières), 5km (3 miles) south of Ronquières village. These include an ascent on the inclined plane on which boats are raised or lowered by 68m (223ft) in tanks on an elevator track.

The South

The worn industrial town of **Binche** boasts one of Europe's most astonishing carnivals, in February, when the masked and fantastically costumed Gilles de Binche turn the streets into a riot of colour in a tradition stretching back to the Spanish conquest of the Incas (Belgium was once a Spanish posses-

Welcome with open arms at the Carnival and Mask Museum

sion). Binche's **Musée International du Carnaval et du Masque** (International Carnival and Mask Museum; open Sun–Thur 9.30am–12.30pm and 1.30–6pm; Sat 1.30–6pm; closed Ash Wednesday and over Christmas; admission fee) in Rue St-Moustier, near the Grand-Place, covers carnival traditions and costumes from around the world, but focuses on the town's own.

A Trappist monk at the Abbey of Our Lady of Scourment

The steam trains of the **Chemin de Fer à Vapeur des Trois Vallées** (Three Valleys Steam Train; runs Apr–Sept; excursion fee), based at Mariembourg in the south of Belgium, bring railway history to life. In the extreme south, in a scenic area called the Botte du Hainaut (Boot of Hainaut), the monks of the **Abbaye Notre-Dame-de-Scourmont** (Abbey of Our Lady of Scourmont) brew Trappist Chimay beer.

MEUSE VALLEY

On its course across Belgium, the River Meuse separates the Ardennes hills and forests from the rolling plains to the west. Pleasant resort towns and scenic countryside are characteristic of the valley.

Liège

Ruled between 980 and 1794 by prince-bishops, Liège was an ecclesiastical city-state. In the end, supporters of the French Revolution burned the city's medieval Gothic

Cathédral St-Lambert (St Lambert's Cathedral). In recent times, Liège has been a declining centre of heavy industry. But the *Cité Ardente* (Hot-Blooded City) supports Belgium's most Mediterranean lifestyle, with no end of fine cafés and restaurants throughout.

The monumental **Palais des Princes-Evêques** (Palace of the Prince-Bishops) in Place St-Lambert in the heart of the city, was once the seat of religious and temporal power and is now Liège's Palais de Justice (Palace of Justice). Begun around 1000 and rebuilt in the 16th century, the palace is the world's largest secular Gothic building. You can visit its porticoed courtyard.

Palace of the Prince-Bishops

Between the palace and the Meuse lies Liège's historic centre. Top billing here goes to the **Musée de la Vie Wallonne** (Museum of Walloon Life; open Tues–Sat 10am–5pm; Sun 10am–4pm; admission fee), in a former Franciscan monastery off Rue Hors-Château. This rambling museum touches on many aspects of Walloon life and culture, from the manufacture of traditional products like porcelain, to cuisine and marionette theatre.

The adjacent **Musée d'Art Religieux et d'Art Mosan** (Museum of Religious and Mosan Art; open Tues–Sat 11am–6pm, Sun 11am–4pm; admission fee) complements this with paintings, sculptures and church vessels and ornamentation in the medieval Meuse Valley style. Further along, Rue Hors-Château begins the **Montagne de Bueren** (Bueren Hill), a long and steep street with 374 steps that leads to the once powerful hilltop **Citadelle**

Georges Simenon (1903–89), who wrote 84 novels featuring the Paris police inspector, Maigret, was born in the city of Liège. Simenon grew up in working-class Outremeuse, and the ambience of this quarter pervades many of the books.

(Citadel), which is now a park with a great view of the city.

Staying on Hors-Château brings you to the Romanesque **Eglise St-Barthélemy** (Church of St Bartholomew; open Mon–Sat 10am–noon and 2–5pm; Sun 2–5pm; admission fee). Inside is a medieval masterpiece, the bronze **Fonts Baptismaux** (Baptismal Font) by Renier de Huy. Created between 1107 and 1118, it is decorated by a scene of Jesus being baptised and has a base supported by 10 sculpted oxen.

On the riverside Quai de Maestricht, a cluster of three museums are being merged to form **Le Grand Curtius**, a museum of Liège art and history scheduled to open in 2007. This renovated complex of historical buildings will include local archaeological finds and decorative art from the **Musée Curtius** (Curtius Museum), beautiful works of glass and porcelain from the **Musée du Verre**, and firearms and other weapons from the **Musée d'Armes** (the latter illustrating the fine craftsmanship that has made Liège a centre for arms manufacture for many centuries). The centrepiece of the new complex is the waterside mansion of the 17th-century arms dealer, Jean Curtius.

With its entrance in Rue Féronstrée, the **Musée de l'Art Wallon** (Museum of Walloon Art; open Tues–Sat 1–6pm; Sun 11am–4.30pm; admission fee) has a small but impressive collection of paintings and sculpture by Walloon artists

from the 16th century to the present, including works by
René Magritte, Paul Delvaux and Félicien Rops.

Further south, on the opposite bank of the river at Quai
Van Beneden, is the **Aquarium et Musée de Zoologie**
(Aquarium and Zoological Museum; open Easter and
July–Aug: Mon–Fri 10am–6pm, Sat–Sun 10.30am–6pm;
other times: Mon–Fri 9am–5pm, Sat–Sun 10.30am–6pm;
admission fee), which has excellent underwater displays and
some rather dusty-looking bird, insect and animal exhibits.

In the **Trésor** (Treasury) of the Gothic **Cathédral St-Paul**
(St Paul's Cathedral; open daily 8am–noon and 2–5pm; admission fee for Treasury), south of the central Carré district,
is the ornate, gold-and-silver **Réliquaire de Charles le
Téméraire** (Reliquary of Charles the Bold) from 1471.

Beautiful, and expensive, **Val-St-Lambert** crystal is produced by hand at a factory (open daily 9am–5pm; admission
fee to workshop) in Rue du Val in the industrial suburb of
Seraing, 5km (3 miles) southwest of Liège. You can watch the
craftspeople at work and buy some of the finished product.

Huy

This small river resort Midway between Liège and Namur
has a clifftop **Citadelle** (Citadel; open Apr–June, Sept:
Mon–Fri 10am–6pm, Sat–Sun 10am–7pm; July–Aug: daily
10am–8pm; admission fee), reached by cable car. In the
town, the 14th-century Gothic **Collégiale Notre-Dame**
(Church of Our Lady; open Sat–Thur 9am–noon and 2–5pm;
church free; admission fee for Treasury) has a fine rose window, Li Rondia. Among the historical and folklore collection
of the **Musée Communal** (Municipal Museum; open
May–Sept: Mon–Fri 2–4pm, Sat–Sun 2–6pm; admission
fee), in a 17th-century Franciscan priory in Rue Vankeer-
berghen, is the exceptional *Beau Dieu de Huy (Good Lord of
Huy)*, a wooden crucifix dating from 1240.

Namur

Capital of Wallonia, this resort town at the confluence of the rivers Meuse and Sambre is dominated by the sprawling defensive works of a fortification that has been developed and expanded over 2,000 years. You can walk or drive up to the summit of the **Citadelle** (Citadel; open permanently; free) on Route Merveilleuse for a superb view over the city and its two rivers. Now a tourist attraction, the former military installations, from the 15th to the 19th centuries, are occupied by restaurants and shops.

Across the Sambre is **Le Corbeil**, the oldest quarter of Namur, where atmospheric streets are filled with restaurants, cafés and shops. Occupying the 15th-century Renaissance former butcher's market in Rue du Pont, the **Musée Archéologique** (Archaeological Museum; open Tues–Fri 10am–5pm, Sat–Sun 10.30am–5pm; admission fee), dis-

Namur's citadel dominates the town and the river

Sculpture group in the Gardens of Annevoie

plays finds from the Gallic, Roman and Frankish periods in the Meuse Valley. Grotesque and erotic, the art of the 19th-century Namur painter Félicien Rops is presented at the **Musée Félicien Rops** (Félicien Rops Museum; open July–Aug: daily 10am–6pm; Sept–June: Tues–Sun 10am–6pm; admission fee) in Rue Fumal.

A bright, domed Italianate construction from 1751, the **Cathédral St-Aubin** (St Aubin's Cathedral), in Place St-Aubin, has paintings by the Rubens School. In the neighbouring **Musée Diocésain** (Diocesan Museum; open Easter–Oct: Tues–Sat 10am–noon and 2.30–6pm, Sun 2.30–6pm; Nov–Easter: Tues–Sun 2.30–4.30pm; admission fee) are religious vestments, sculptures and reliquaries.

On the riverside road between Namur and Dinant, 2km (1 mile) inland from Annevoie-Rouillon, is the imposing 18th-century **Château d'Annevoie** and its magnificent **Jardins d'Annevoie** (Gardens of Annevoie; open July–Aug: daily 9.30am–6.30pm; Apr–June and Sept–Nov: until 5.30pm; admission fee). An extensive array of fountains, fish-ponds, canals and streams is fed with water from the fast-flowing Annevoie stream.

Inland, through the valley of the Molignée stream, 4km (2.5 miles) from the stone-built village of Denée, is the 19th-century, neo-Gothic **Abbaye de Maredsous** (Maredsous Abbey; open daily 9am–6pm; free). The twin-towered

Benedictine abbey is set in a forest and visitors come to experience its tranquillity and to sample artisanal beer, cheese and bread.

Dinant

A bustling riverside resort, Dinant was the birthplace of Adolphe Sax (1814–94), the inventor of the saxophone, and is noted for its hand-beaten copperware, known as *dinanderie*.

Dominating the town from a clifftop on the right bank of the Meuse, and accessible by cable car, Dinant's **Citadelle** (Citadel; open Apr–Sept: daily 10am–6pm; Oct–Mar: Sat–Thur 10am–4.30pm; admission fee) has seen many conquerors come and go. Appropriately, it houses exhibits on weapons and warfare. The 17th-century **Collégiale Notre-Dame** (Church of Notre-Dame), beside the river, with its striking bulbous spire, is a symbol of the town.

On the edge of Dinant, at the **Abbaye de Leffe** (Leffe Abbey), the potent Leffe beer is brewed. The 16th-century **Château de Freÿr** (Freÿr Castle; open July–Aug: Tues–Sun 11am–12.45pm and 2.15–5.45pm; Apr–June, Sept: Sat–Sun; admission fee) and its ornamental gardens stand beside the river, 6km (4 miles) to the south.

Dinant with the Church of Notre-Dame

THE ARDENNES

The sparsely populated Ardennes, a region of hills, forests and steep river valleys between the Meuse and the German border, is Belgium's great outdoors. In autumn the forests are a blaze of colour. The Ardennes is criss-crossed by rivers – streams, really – that wind through steep-sided gorges and occasionally tumble over waterfalls or form bubbling rapids.

Bouillon

In the valley of the fast-flowing River Semois, **Bouillon** is dominated by the powerful battlements of **Château de Bouillon** (Bouillon Castle; open Dec–Feb: Mon–Fri 1–5pm, Sat–Sun 10am–5pm; Mar and Oct–Nov: daily 10am–5pm; Apr–June and Sept: Mon–Fri 10am–6pm, Sat–Sun 10am–7pm; July–Aug: daily 10am–7pm; admission fee), from the 12th century but with later additions. The wildly looping Semois outside town is great for fishing, and the riverbank offers good hiking.

Renowned for its locally produced Trappist beer and cheese, the Cistercian **Abbaye d'Orval** (Orval Abbey; open June–Sept: daily 9.30am–6.30pm; Oct and Mar–May: daily 9.30am–6pm; Nov–Feb: daily 10.30am–5.30pm; admission fee), east of Bouillon near Villers-devant-Orval, dates from medieval times, but a 20th-century reconstruction now occupies the site.

Stained glass at Orval Abbey

East of Orval, **Arlon** is in the Belgian province of Luxembourg, close to the border with the Grand Duchy of Luxembourg. Its **Musée Luxembourgeois** (Luxembourg Museum; open Mon–Sat 9am–noon and 1.30–5.30pm; mid-Apr–mid-Sept: also Sun 1.30–5.30pm; admission fee), in Rue des Martyrs, displays items from the area's Gallic, Roman and Frankish periods.

Bastogne

North of Arlon, **Bastogne** was rebuilt after being heavily damaged in World War II during the Battle of the Ardennes. Besieged in the town, US general Anthony McAuliffe replied succinctly to a German surrender demand: 'Nuts'. On the Colline du Mardasson, 3km (2 miles) east of Bastogne, the star-shaped **Mardasson Monument** is a memorial to the Americans killed in the battle. In the on-site **Bastogne Historical Centre** (open daily; admission fee),

Battle of the Bulge

In December 1944, the 'Ghost Front' among the misty, snow-covered forests along the German frontier in the Ardennes had been quiet for three months. Soldiers manning the thinly-stretched American lines in this backwater of the war thought themselves fortunate. They were wrong.

Before dawn on 16 December a massive artillery barrage was followed by waves of attacking German tanks and troops, heading for the River Meuse. The shape of the German penetration gave the Ardennes Offensive its popular name: the Battle of the Bulge. Heavy fighting halted the advance, and reinforcements pushed the German army back. By February, the battle in the devastated Ardennes was over. Some 80,000 Americans and 100,000 Germans paid the price. The scars of war have healed. Memorials, inscriptions and tanks on concrete plinths are the only visible signs of the drama that once brought the Ardennes brutally to the world's attention.

La Roche-en-Ardenne beneath its ruined castle

film material and graphical presentations illustrate the course of the fighting, and a collection of military equipment and uniforms from the period adds historical depth.

La Roche-en-Ardenne and St-Hubert

Northwest of Bastogne, where a bend of the River Ourthe courses through a deep valley, **La Roche-en-Ardenne** has a ruined 11th-century castle on a steep hill above the town. To the southwest, **St-Hubert** is a small market town at the heart of the Ardennes game-hunting region. Its 16th-century **Basilique St-Hubert** (St Hubert's Basilica), in Place de la Basilique, is an impressive mix of Romanesque and Gothic. The nearby **Musée de la Vie Rurale en Wallonie** (Museum of Rural Life in Wallonia; open Mar–Apr and Sept–Nov: daily 10am–5pm; May–Aug: until 6.30pm; admission fee), at Fourneau St-Michel, is an open-air museum, containing examples of traditional Ardennes houses and workshops.

The **Euro Space Centre** (open daily 10am–5pm; admission fee), northwest of St-Hubert, near Transinne, is more than a museum containing exhibits on space exploration. It's also a training environment for enthusiasts, budding astronauts and business executives seeking to hone their project-management skills. Nearby **Redu**, the 'village of books', has been taken over by second-hand bookshops and a supporting cast of shops selling craft items and locally produced food and drinks.

Han-sur-Lesse

North of Redu, the **Parc Naturel de Lesse et Lomme** (Lesse and Lomme Nature Park) is set in beautiful scenery between the rivers Lesse and Lomme. Its focal point is the village of **Han-sur-Lesse**. Reached by guided tour from the village, the spectacular **Grottes de Han** (Han Caves; open May–June, Sept–Oct: daily 10am–noon and 1.30–4.30pm; July–Aug: until 5pm; admission fee; <www. grotte-de-han.be>) is a vast underground cavern complex through which runs the River Lesse. Also reached by guided tour from Han-sur-Lesse, the **Réserve d'Animaux Sauvages** (Wild Animal Reserve; open daily; admission fee), is a wildlife park with aurochs, bears, bison, deer, wild boar and wild horses.

Inside the Han Caves

To the west, the moated 12th-century **Château Féodal** (Feudal Castle; open daily Apr–Sept: 9am–6pm; Oct–Mar: 9am–5pm; admission fee) at **Lavaux-Ste-Anne** houses the **Musée de la Chasse et de la Conservation de la Nature** (Museum of Hunting and Nature Conservation), filled with animal

skulls and trophies. Westwards in the direction of Dinant, the walls and towers of romantic, medieval **Château de Vêves** (Vêves Castle; open for guided tours May–Sept: daily 10am–6pm; Apr and Oct–Nov: until 5pm; admission fee) loom above a landscape of forests and valleys.

Further north, **Durbuy** owes its isolation and the drama of its location to the River Ourthe, which flows through a deep valley in which the town lies. A 17th-century château, and viewpoints on the surrounding cliffs add to the scenic attractions of this popular destination. The vicinity of the nearby **Wéris** is dotted with Stone-Age megaliths.

Spa

The healthy properties of the mineral springs around the elegant small town of **Spa** have been appreciated since ancient times. In the 18th and 19th centuries, well-heeled visitors

Local produce in Durbuy

came to take the waters, stroll in the forests, and to gamble and relax. Spa has lost much of its exclusive cachet since then, but has reinvented itself as a wellness resort. The centrepiece of Spa's regeneration is the **Thermes de Spa** (open Sun–Thur 9am–8pm, Fri–Sat 9am–10pm; admission fee), a modern thermal centre that replaces the 1869 Etablisse-

Modern Thermes de Spa

ment des Bains. Located on a hill above the town, and reached by a new funicular, the centre has large outdoor and indoor pools fed by natural Spa Clementine mineral water.

Beside the old baths is the **Casino**, from 1763, and the **Theatre**, both signs of the town's racy *belle époque* reputation.

Pouhon is the Walloon word for an iron-rich spring, and the **Pouhon Pierre le Grand** (Peter the Great Spring; open daily 9am–6pm; free) in Place Pierre le Grand is a pavilion built over such a spring. Named after the Russian Tsar who took the cure at Spa, the pavilion served formerly as a winter garden and is now a venue for art exhibitions.

Also worth visiting is the bottling plant of **Spa Monopole** (open for guided tours Mon–Fri 9am–5pm; free), the company that commercially exploits the town's mineral waters, beside the railway station.

The **Route des Fontaines** (Promenade of the Springs) is a tour of the various mineral springs in the hills and forest around Spa. These are the Fontaine de Barisart, where Spa Barisart originates; the Fontaine de la Géronstère, in a garden grotto; the side-by-side Fontaine de la Sauvenière and Fontaine de Groesbeek, in an underground vault; and the

Fontaine du Tonnelet. Also outside Spa, 3km (2 miles) to the north, is the **Lac de Warfaaz**, a small lake with a cluster of cafés and restaurants, and pedal-boats for hire in summer.

OSTKANTONE (EAST CANTONS)

This scenic district of about 100,000 inhabitants, two-thirds of whom are German-speakers, is in the far east of Belgium. The landscape can be characterised as sub-Alpine, but as with the Ardennes in general it is hilly rather than mountainous.

With a population of 17,000, **Eupen** is the main town of the East Cantons and the seat of the district's **Exekutive** (Parliament), housed in a mansion from 1761, in Klötzer-bahn. Also in the town centre, the baroque **Sankt-Nikolaus-Pfarrkirche** (St Nicholas's Church), from the 1720s, has twin towers with bulbous spires.

The resort village of **Malmédy** on the Amblève is known for its costumed carnival. **Lac de Robertville** (Robertville Lake), south of Robertville, has beaches, swimming and pedal-boats. East of here, **Stausee Bütgenbach** (Bütgenbach Lake), just outside **Bütgenbach**, has a sports centre, a caravan and chalet park, and boating.

The pastoral Our Valley

Medieval **Burg Reinhardstein** (Reinhardstein Castle; open for guided tours mid-June–mid-Sept: Sun 2.15–5.15pm; July–Aug: Tues, Thur, Sat 3.30pm; admission fee), on a defensible position above the River Warche near Robertville, was owned by the Metternich family, among whose scions was the distinguished Napoleonic-era Austrian statesman.

On a hill above the rugged valley of the River Our, which flows along the border with Germany, a ruined 10th-century **Burg** (Castle; open Sat–Sun and holidays 10am–6pm; free) looks down on the whitewashed houses of **Burg-Reuland**. Inside the village's 17th-century **Sankt-Stephanus-Kirche** (St Stephen's Church) in Dorfstrasse, recumbent images of Baron Balthasar von Pallant and his wife Elisabeth have been carved on their black schist sarcophagus.

> On several days a month between April and October, the steam trains and 1930s carriages of the Vennbahn run from Bütgenbach through the north of the East Cantons, into Germany, and back again.

Hautes Fagnes/Höhes Venn (High Fens)

Belgium's largest nature reserve covers a high plateau of moorland and morass between Eupen and Robertville, valued for its unique and fragile sub-Alpine flora and fauna. A network of wooden boardwalks crosses the moors, affording an easy way to penetrate a landscape that stemmed from the retreating glaciers of the last Ice Age.

There are two main entrances to the **Hautes Fagnes**. At **Baraque-Michel**, there is a car park, a restaurant and the Fischbach-Kapelle, a chapel from 1830. Mont-Rigi has a restaurant and a research station. Behind this is the **Fagne de la Poleûr**, part of the reserve's peripheral zone, through which wends a wooden walkway for tours that provide an introduction to the Hautes Fagnes while sparing more critical areas.

South of here, the **Signal de Botrange** marks Belgium's highest point, 694m (2,276ft) above sea level. Off the N676 between Mont-Rigi and Sourbrodt is the **Centre Nature de Botrange** (Botrange Nature Centre; open daily 10am–6pm; admission fee), with a cafeteria, shop, information centre and exhibition area. Guided tours of the reserve leave from here.

WHAT TO DO

PARTICIPANT SPORTS

Mountain-bikes are widely available for hire from private companies in the Ardennes, where much of the terrain – rough hills, narrow forest trails, unbridged streams – is well-suited to mountain-biking. More information is available from the Ligue Vélocipédique Belge, Avenue du Globe 49, 1190 Brussels, tel: (02) 349 19 11.

Hiking: Long-distance hiking routes criss-cross the country. These are known as the Sentiers des Grandes Randonnées in Wallonia, and the Grote Routepaden/Lange Afstandswandelwegen in Flanders. Mountaineering in the strict sense of the term does not exist, but there is stiff rock-climbing on riverside cliffs up to 100m (330ft) high in the Meuse Valley, with those at Anseremme near Dinant being quite tough.

Golf: Some 50 golf courses afford an adequate choice, and at most clubs visitors can either take a temporary membership or pay green-fees. Brussels: Royal Waterloo Golf Club, Vieux Chemin de Wavre 50, Ohain, tel: (02) 633 18 50; Royal Tervuren Golf Club, Kasteel Ravenstein, Tervuren, tel: (02) 767 58 01. Ardennes: Durbuy Golf Club, Route d'Oppagne, Barvaux, tel: (086) 21 44 54; Royal Hautes Fagnes Golf Club, Balmoral, Spa, tel: (087) 79 30 30. Coast: Royal Zoute Golf Club, Caddiespad 14, Knokke-Zoute, tel: (050) 60 12 27. More information is available from the Fédération Royale Belge de Golf, Chaussée de la Hulpe 110, 1050 Brussels, tel: (02) 672 23 89.

Tennis is popular and courts, indoor and open-air, abound. Contact the Fédération Royale Belge de Tennis, Galerie de la Porte Louise 203/3, 1050 Brussels, tel: (02) 548 03 04.

Horse-riding is widely available. In Flanders you are likely to be riding in flat, open country; in Wallonia, in hilly, forested country. Brussels has good horse-riding paths in the Forêt de Soignes. More information is available from the Fédération Royale Belge des Sports Equestres, Avenue Houba de Strooper 156, 1020 Brussels, tel: (02) 478 50 56.

Watersports: In addition to the extensive facilities on the coast for yachting, power-boating and windsurfing, Belgium's rivers, canals and lakes afford sailing possibilities. More information is available from the Verbond van Vlaamse Watersportverenigingen, Beatrijslaan 25, 2050 Antwerp, tel: (03) 219 69 67.

Canoeing: Canoeists have plenty of choice and a fair amount of action on Ardennes rivers. There are few really worthwhile rapids – though there are some – but in spring, when the snows melt, the water can often be fast-flowing and occasionally rough. The descent of the River Lesse is a popular day out for people of any age. Other good canoeing rivers are the Amblève and the Our.

Snow Time

Snow is probable in the Ardennes in winter, though it's unpredictable and not guaranteed. There are about a dozen downhill skiing areas with lifts, but most pistes are not long and none are overly challenging. Cross-country skiing is more popular – or at least there are far more possibilities and more likelihood of being able to do it. Some of the best cross-country skiing, on prepared pistes, is in the Hautes Fagnes. The Ardennes region is easily accessible from other parts of Belgium, so a skiing break can be had at short notice. Skis and other equipment can be hired from sports shops and hotels in the main skiing areas.

Snow reports are issued by the Touring Club, tel: (02) 233 24 90. More information is available from local tourist offices in the Ardennes and from the Belgian National Tourist Office, Rue du Marché-aux-Herbes 63, 1000 Brussels, tel: (02) 504 03 90.

Parachutists and sky-divers take to the air from an airfield outside Spa in the Ardennes. Instruction is on offer for beginners. More information is available from More information is available from the Royal Aero-Para Club de Spa, Aérodrome de Spa, Route de la Sauvenière, tel : (087) 77 41 83.

Bicycling in the Ardennes

SPECTATOR SPORTS

Football is the top spectator sport, with clubs such as FC Anderlecht, Club Brugge and Standard Liège invariably in contention for national honours and liable to make some progress in European competitions. The national side rejoices in the nickname 'Red Devils'. International matches are played at the King Baudouin Stadium at Heysel, beside the Bruparck recreation centre in Brussels.

Cycle racing is not far behind soccer. Among the internationally respected Belgian competitions are the Toer van Vlaanderen (Tour of Flanders) and the Flèche Wallonne (Walloon Arrow), both in the spring. The Tour de Belgique follows in August, and the Eddy Merckx Grand Prix – named after the great Belgian cycling champion whose nickname was 'the Cannibal' – in September.

In athletics, the Ivo Van Damme Memorial is one of the international prestige meetings, attracting top track and field competitors. The Belgian Classic golf competition, generally played at Royal Tervuren, attracts top competitors, as do the Belgian Open and the Antwerp Classic in tennis.

In the Brussels area there are horse-racing tracks at Groenendaal, G.B. Charlielaan 20, Hoeilaart, tel: (02) 657

30 63, and Sterrebeek, Du Roy de Blicquylaan 43, Sterrebeek, tel: (02) 767 54 75. At Ostend on the North Sea coast is the Wellington Renbaan, Koningin Astridlaan, tel: (059) 80 60 55).

The testing Spa-Francorchamps motor- and motorbike-racing circuit winds among the Ardennes hills and forests between Francorchamps, Malmédy and Stavelot. Belgium's Formula One motor-racing grand prix has been run here, but there is uncertainty about its future due to legal difficulties with tobacco advertising and sponsorship. Another racing circuit is at Heusden-Zolder, in the Kempen near Hasselt.

SHOPPING

Brussels and Antwerp are the country's shopping capitals, rival citadels of style. Bruges has adapted to the lucrative tourist trade, with lace and small speciality shops and souvenir shops throughout the centre. Ghent has a bigger shopping centre, with more of a city ambience to it. Among the coastal resorts, ritzy Knokke-Heist stands out for its many designer boutiques.

Lace Society

Belgium has a tradition of making lace – a threadwork of silk, linen or cotton – that stretches back to the 16th century in Flanders. Brussels and Bruges are the principal sales points. Mechelen, Antwerp, Sint-Truiden, Turnhout, Poperinge and Binche were all at one time, and to a minor extent still are, centres of lace production.

Beware of cheap machine-made and imported imitations, unless you only want a simple souvenir. Belgian handmade lace is expensive, but if you like lace this is the only sort worth buying. It should always be clearly labelled as having been handmade in Belgium.

Good Buys

Regional and local speciality products are generally available at shops and markets around the country, but some can be obtained only in and around their home-base.

Chocolates: The finest Belgian handmade pralines are little short of heavenly – if short at all. You can buy boxes, pre-packed or filled with your own choices from

Chocolates galore

the display shelves in specialist shops (choosing for yourself probably means the chocolates will be fresher). Léonidas, Neuhaus and Godiva are three among many reputable brands. Bear in mind that these chocolates are made with fresh ingredients, like cream, so it's best to eat them fairly soon after you buy them.

Beer and Gin: The range of Belgian beers is vast, so it makes sense to buy those you have tried and liked rather than risk being disappointed by an unknown. Supermarkets stock a reasonable choice and at lower prices than you pay elsewhere. Like Scotland's malt whiskies, Belgian *genièvre/jenever* (gin, or geneva) is a devotee's drink, with hundreds of labels to choose from, all sold in distinctive bottles.

Food: Belgium is justly celebrated for its *pâtisserie*, cheeses, *jambon d'Ardenne* (cured ham) and waffles, among other products. If you can, buy these from speciality shops.

Antiques: These are sold at markets in Brussels, Bruges, Antwerp, Spa and other towns, and in intimidatingly expensive-looking shops.

Diamonds: Antwerp accounts for half of the world's sales of polished diamonds, and visiting the city's Diamond Quarter

Hats off to Belgium's stallholders

(*see page 42*) is fascinating. The 'Antwerp cut' is said to give the stones more sparkle. Quality is guaranteed; bargains aren't.

Crystal: At its workshop outside Liège, Val-St-Lambert, founded in 1826, produces expensive hand-blown and engraved pieces of superior quality.

Metalwork: Look for ornaments and household objects made from *dinanderie*, hand-beaten copper from Dinant on the River Meuse, and pewter from the nearby town of Huy.

Markets

Belgium has street markets of all kinds – craft markets, antiques markets, flea markets, food markets, fish markets, flower markets. They are popular, provide value for money and make for a distinctive shopping experience.

Among the best in Brussels is the raggedy Vieux Marché (Old Market) flea market (daily 7am–2pm) in Place du Jeu de Balle in the Marolles district. Far more sophisticated, and expensive, is the Antiques Market (Sat 9am–6pm, Sun 9am–2pm) in Place du Grand-Sablon. Jewellery, ornaments and other bits and pieces are sold in laid-back style at the Crafts Market (Sat–Sun 10am–6pm) in Place de l'Agora. The Grand-Place is the setting for a small but colourful Flower Market (Tues–Sun 10am–6pm). Products from North Africa are a key ingredient of the Midi Market (Sun 5am–1pm), a general street market around Gare du Midi.

In Antwerp, a general street market takes place in Vrijdagmarkt (Wed and Fri 8am–1pm). The Antiques Market (Easter–Oct: Sat 9am–5pm) in Lijnwaadmarkt, near the cathedral, includes plain old junk alongside genuine antiques. Once a year, the Grote Markt is taken over by the Rubens Market (15 Aug, all day), its stallholders dressed in 17th-century costume.

The biggest general street market (Sat 7am–1pm) in Bruges is in 't Zand and Beursplein. A close second is the weekly general street market (Sat 7am–1pm) in the Markt. The Dijver canalside is the setting for a fine antiques and flea market (mid-Mar–mid-Nov: Sat–Sun noon–5pm). Ghent's flea market (Fri–Sun 7am–1pm) is in Bij St Jacobs and Beverhoutplein, and there's a flower market (daily 7am–1pm) in Kouter.

Liège's Marché de la Batte street market (Sun 8am–2pm) on Quai de la Batte beside the Meuse is among the most famous in Belgium. Spa has a small outdoor antiques and flea market (Sun 8am–2pm) in the Galerie Léopold II at the Parc de Sept Heures, and Tongeren has an enormous flea market (Sun 7am–1pm) held under the old town walls.

Market produce

NIGHTLIFE AND ENTERTAINMENT

Eating and drinking are the chief pleasures, but they're by no means the only ones. What's on information can be found in the weekly English-language magazine, *The Bulletin*, and in the daily newspapers *Le Soir* and *De Standaard* – in French and Dutch respectively but the listings are fairly easy to follow even for people who don't speak the language. Tourist offices can provide information on cultural events and venues in their area.

Brussels and Antwerp have the most nightlife and entertainment options, followed by Ghent and Liège. Bruges is not notable in this respect, though the town is far from dead after dark.

Cinemas: Most films are shown in their original language in Brussels and Flanders (invariably English, with a smattering of French and Dutch films), with subtitles in French and Dutch. Cinemas in Wallonia often show mainstream English films dubbed into French, while the few cinemas in the East Cantons are likely to screen films in German. The bigger cities have multi-screen cinemas.

Casinos: These are located in resort towns at the coast, along the River Meuse and in the Ardennes. Coast: Zeedijk 150, Blankenberge, tel: (050) 41 93 93; Zeedijk-Albertstrand 509, Knokke-Heist, tel: (050) 63 05 00; Monacoplein, Ostend, tel: (059) 70 51 11. Meuse: Esplanade 1, Chaudfontaine, tel: (41) 65 07 41; Avenue Baron de Moreau 1, Namur, tel: (081) 22 30 21; Boulevard des Souverains 6, Dinant, tel: (082) 69 84 84. Ardennes: Rue Royale 4, Spa, tel: (087) 77 20 54.

Performing Arts
Brussels
Classical Music, Opera and Ballet: The neoclassical Théâtre Royal de la Monnaie, Place de la Monnaie, tel: (02) 229 12 00,

Théâtre Royal de la Monnaie in Brussels

is the home of the Royal Monnaie Opera and the modern dance group Rosas. The Palais des Beaux-Arts (Bozar), Rue Ravenstein 23, tel: (02) 507 82 00, is home to the Belgian National Orchestra. The city's main venue for chamber music is the Conservatoire Royal de Musique, Rue de la Régence 30, tel: (02) 511 04 27. Cirque Royal, Rue de l'Enseignement 81, tel: (02) 218 20 15, also hosts theatre, dance, jazz and rock.

Theatre: The elegant Théâtre Royal du Parc, Rue de la Loi 3, tel: (02) 505 30 30, puts on mainstream theatre. Modern theatre and dance are at Théâtre Varia, Rue du Sceptre 78, tel: (02) 640 82 58. For sophisticated marionette theatre in Brussels dialect, visit Théâtre Toone VII, Impasse Schuddeveld, Petite Rue des Bouchers 21, tel: (02) 513 54 86, attached to a traditional café.

Rock and Pop: Forest National, Avenue du Globe 36, tel: (02) 347 03 55, is the place for concerts by big-name performers, both national and international.

Sculpture at the Joseph Rylandt Hall, a concert venue in Bruges

Antwerp: De Opera, Frankrijklei 3, tel: (070) 22 02 02, is home to the Koninklijke Vlaamse Opera (Royal Flemish Opera) and is a regular venue for the Koninklijk Ballet van Vlaanderen (Royal Flanders Ballet). The Koningin Elisabethzaal, Koningin Astridplein 23–24, tel: (03) 233 84 44, is used for classical and rock music, and theatre. deSingel, Desguinlei 25, tel: (03) 248 28 28, a multipurpose arts centre, for mostly modern dance, opera, theatre and more. From mid-June to mid-September the cathedral carillon plays concerts which can be appreciated from any point on the street around the centre. The Arenberg Theater, Arenbergstraat 28, tel: (070) 22 21 92, occasionally puts on productions in English.

Ghent: The Koninklijke Opera, Schouwburgstraat 3, tel: (09) 268 10 11, hosts opera and ballet.

Bruges: The modern Concertgebouw, 't Zand, tel: (070) 22 33 02, hosts classical music, opera, dance, as well as a wide range of musical genres from jazz to pop and world music. Prior to its opening (in 2002), the Koninklijke Stadsschouwburg, Vlamingstraat 29, tel: (050) 44 30 60, was the city's main cultural venue. Another important concert hall in Bruges is the Joseph Ryelandt Hall at Achiel Van Ackerplein.

Liège: The city's main concert venue is the Conservatoire Royal de Musique, Boulevard Piercot 27–29, tel: (04) 222 03 06. The Théâtre Royal de Liège, Rue des Dominicains 1, tel: (04) 221 47 20, is the home of the highly regarded Opéra Royal de Wallonie (Royal Wallonia Opera).

BELGIUM FOR CHILDREN

Children have plenty to do in Belgium, choosing from a variety of museums, theme-parks and outdoor pursuits.

Museums: Among things with specific appeal for children are: Musée des Enfants (Children's Museum), Rue du Bourgmestre 15, Brussels, tel: (02) 640 01 07; Musée du Jouet (Toy Museum), Rue de l'Association 24, Brussels, tel: (02) 219 61 68; dinosaur skeletons at the Musée des Sciences Naturelles (Natural History Museum), Rue Vautier 29, Brussels, tel: (02) 627 42 38; vintage horse-drawn and electric trams at the Musée du Transport Urbain (City Transport Museum), Avenue de Tervuren 364b, Brussels, tel: (02) 515 31 08; more toys at the superb Speelgoedmuseum Mechelen (Mechelen Toy Museum), Nekkerspoel 21, Mechelen, tel: (015) 55 70 75; and the model buildings of Antwerpse Miniatuurstad (Antwerp Miniature City), Hangar 15a, Scheldekaaien, Antwerp, tel: (03) 237 03 29.

Nature Parks: Children can get close to nature in a safe environment at: Dierenpark Planckendael (Planckendael Wildlife Park), Leuvensesteenweg 582, Muizen-Mechelen, tel: (015) 41 49 21, a wildlife and

Bokrijk open-air museum

country park near Mechelen; Vlindertuin (Butterfly Garden), Bronlaan 14, Knokke-Heist, tel: (050) 61 04 72, beside Het Zwin Nature Reserve; Monde Sauvage Safari (Wild Safari World), Fange de Deigné 3, Deigné-Aywaille, tel: (04) 360 90 70, in the Ardennes south of Liège, with wild animals ranging from lions and tigers to goats and donkeys; Crête des Cerfs (Stags' Crest), Bouillon, tel: (061) 46 71 52, a park with small animals such as deer and their fawns; and the Ferme de Dry Hamptay (Dry Hamptay Farm), Rue des Grottes 46, Han-sur-Lesse, tel: (084) 37 82 31, a children's farm.

Theme Parks: Rides, cartoon characters and fairground attractions, together with the associated Aqualibi water park, are at Walibi Belgium, Wavre (just outside Brussels), tel: (010) 42 15 00; also not far from Brussels is the Recreatiepark 't Zoet Water, Noëstraat 15, Oud-Heverlee, tel: (016) 47 75 55, which is designed for small children; Boudewijn Seapark, A De Baeckerstraat 12, Bruges, tel: (050) 38 38 38, is an attractions park which also hosts the dolphin and seal shows of the Dolfinarium; Bellewaerde, Meenseweg 497, near Ypres, tel: (057) 46 86 86, is a park with rides and other attractions, set amid the former battlefields of World War I; Plopsaland, De Pannelaan 68, Adinkerke-De Panne, tel: (058) 42 02 02, is an amusement park for small children, close to the seaside; Telecoo, Coo, tel: (080) 68 42 65), features attractions and a chairlift located beside the Amblève River in the Ardennes.

Other Attractions

In the Where to Go section are details of: Autoworld, the Belgian Comic Strip Centre and Mini-Europe in Brussels; Antwerp Zoo; Bokrijk Open-air Museum in the Kempen; and the Euro Space Center in the Ardennes. In addition, there are the North Sea beaches; horse-and-carriage tours; canal and river tours by boat; and puppet theatres in some towns.

Calendar of Events

The following is a brief guide to major events. More information is available from the national and local tourist offices.

January Ronse: Festival of Fools.

February Binche: Carnival of the Gilles. Malmédy: Carnival of the Banes Courants and Haguètes. Eupen: Carnival and Rosenmontag cortège.

March Brussels: International Fantasy Film Festival. Ostend: Bal du Rat Mort (Dead Rat Ball) Carnival. Fosses-la-Ville: Carnival of the Chinels. Stavelot: Carnival of the Blancs Moussis.

April Leuven: International Folklore Festival. Hasselt: Meieavondviering (May Day's Eve Festival). Ghent: Floraliën (Flower Festival; 2010).

May Brussels: Queen Elisabeth International Music Competition; Brussels Jazz Rally. Bruges: Procession of the Holy Blood. Ypres (Ieper): Kattestoet (Festival of the Cats; 2006, 2009). Mons: Car d'Or (Golden Chariot) cortège and Lumeçon (St George and the Dragon) pageant.

June Knokke-Heist: International Cartoon Festival. Oostduinkerke: Shrimp Festival. Oudenaarde: Beer Festival. Tournai: Day of the Four Processions.

July Brussels: Ommegang, recreation of a 16th-century procession, in the Grand-Place; National Day Parade, 21 July. Ghent: Gentse Feesten (Ghent Festivities), a music, cultural and street festival. Veurne: Boetprocessie (Procession of the Penitents).

August Brussels: biennial Carpet of Flowers in Grand-Place; Planting of the Meiboom (May Tree) in Grand-Place. Leuven: Marktrock Music Festival. Bruges: Reiefeest (Canals Festival; 2007, 2010); Praalstoet van de Gouden Boom (Golden Tree Pageant; 2007). Mechelen: International Carillon Competition. Zeebrugge: Sand Sculpture Festival at the beach. Knokke-Heist: Blessing of the Sea. Liège: Outremeuse Folklore Festival.

September Poperinge: Hops Festival. Tournai: Procession of the Plague.

October Ghent: Flanders International Film Festival.

November Bruges: International Antiques Fair. Ypres (Ieper): Armistice Day commemoration, 11 November.

December Brussels, Bruges and Ghent: Christmas markets. Bruges: Snow and Ice Sculpture Festival. Bastogne: Walnut Fair.

EATING OUT

Eating and drinking go a long way towards defining the national lifestyle, and Belgians take their dining pleasures seriously. Their cuisine is regional and unpretentious, based on the country's local products and specialities, and most of it is of excellent quality. Portions are generous. Although the regional cuisines are strongly defined, in the cities at least you should have no trouble sampling dishes from all over Belgium. A new generation of chefs has begun blurring some of the old regional distinctions, creating a fusion of dishes and ingredients (and incorporating ingredients from beyond Belgium's borders).

The Ardennes has a deserved reputation for the quality of its food products. *Jambon d'Ardenne* (Ardennes ham), Ardennes pâté and fresh-caught river trout (when it can be found, since much of the trout served is farmed) are among the delicacies produced in this region, and the town of Bouillon must have done something right to have given its name to the clear beef, chicken or vegetable soups that are a common starter at meal-times. On the coast, grey North Sea shrimps are considered a delicacy – at Oostduinkerke fishermen still harvest them off the beach using 'seagoing' horses – and in the spring, herring (*hareng/haring* or *maatjes*), lightly salted on the boats, is filleted and eaten raw. Brussels has a tradition of making stews and sauces with the local *gueuze* beers.

Mussels are a great favourite

Lunch in the Galerie St-Hubert

Restaurants

The word 'restaurant' can mean anything from a formal, top-class establishment to a small café. Even the bigger railway stations and department stores have acceptable restaurants. Many waiters speak English and menus are often printed in a variety of languages. At lunch *(dejeuner/middagmaal)* and dinner *(diner/avondeten)*, there is frequently a tourist menu *(menu touristique/toeristenmenu)*, or a dish of the day *(plat du jour/dagschotel)*, or menu of the day *(menu du jour/dagmenu)*; these represent the best value.

Bars and cafés usually serve snacks in the morning and lunch from noon; some serve dinner in the late afternoon and evening, too.

Value-added tax, or VAT (TVA/BTW), is included in the bill. A service charge is usually incorporated too, and in this case there's no need to leave a separate tip unless you want to, but it is customary to leave at least the small change.

Breakfast

Most hotels serve a substantial buffet breakfast *(petit deje-uner/ontbijt)*, which can see you through until lunchtime with no trouble at all. Along with tea and coffee or fruit juice, there will be a variety of breads, cheeses and cold meats, plus fresh fruit and cereal, yogurt and fruit salad, buns and pastries. You may be asked if you would like a boiled egg, and some hotels provide buffet grills, so you can have a fried breakfast as well. Even in the smaller hotels the choice is usually large and the food fresh. A few hotels serve a full American or English breakfast. Some provide only a Continental breakfast of coffee or tea, and a croissant and jam, that is scarcely worth the time it takes to eat. Breakfast is usually included in the room rate, but not always, particularly in the more expensive hotels.

Cold Dishes and Snacks

A *sandwich/boterham* is an open sandwich that's served in many cafés and snackbars. Generally comprising two or three large slices of bread, or a large section of a French loaf *(baguette/stokbrood)*, with the filling of your choice, and perhaps accompanied by a salad, they are usually substantial and good value. There is an enormous range: fish, meat,

---

Belgian Fries

The not-so-humble Belgian french fries *(frites/frieten)* – which Belgians maintain should, by right of primogeniture, actually be called just Belgian fries – are twice-fried to hold in the flavour. Fries are invariably topped with any one of a variety of calorie-laden sauces, of which mayonnaise is the most popular, but which can be ketchup, mustard, curry and others. Almost every neighbourhood and village has its own stall *(friterie/frituur)*.

cheese and salad. Bars generally serve light snacks like *croque monsieur* (a toasted ham and cheese sandwich) and spaghetti bolognese.

Fish and Shellfish

You can eat fish at many restaurants, but naturally seafood predominates in the coastal resorts, as does freshwater fish in towns and villages beside the Ardennes rivers (though most of the river trout is farmed). Mussels (despite the fact that they

Fish at the market

come from neighbouring Holland), are a great favourite when they're in season, from about mid-July to mid-February. They are generally served steamed in a large pot, or in white wine, and accompanied by various sauces and by french fries.

Trout *(truite/forel)* is served in a white-wine sauce, and boiled eel *(anguilles/paling)* in a green herb sauce as *anguilles au vert/paling in 't groen*. North Sea sole is generally served grilled with a butter sauce, or with a creamy sauce as *sole à l'Ostendaise/zeetong op Oostendse wijze*. A few restaurants still serve the traditional Ghent soup-like stew *waterzooï op Gentse wijze* with the freshwater fish that were its original prime ingredient, alongside vegetables, but since most rivers are now too polluted to permit this, chicken is invariably substituted.

Meat and Poultry

Beef, pork and chicken play a prominent role on Belgian menus. Steak and french fries is a hardy standby in many restaurants. Watch out for *filet américain*, which might conjure up a mouth-watering image of a Texas T-bone steak, but is in fact raw minced beef mixed with chopped onions. A classic dish of braised beef casseroled in beer, onions and herbs is called *carbonnades à la Flamande/karbonaden op zijn Vlaams*. *Stoemp* is a mixture of mashed potatoes and other vegetables, served with sausage, a chop, or some other kind of meat. Veal *(veau/kalf)* tastes good as *ragoût liégois*, a simple stew of potatoes, vegetables and veal, and liver *(foie/lever)* dishes are widely available.

Game

During the eagerly awaited autumn hunting season in the Ardennes, game *(gibier/wild)* appears on menus all over Belgium, but naturally more so in the Ardennes – going there for a short culinary vacation called a *weekend gastronomique* is close to being a national cult activity. Among the dishes are rabbit or hare cooked in naturally fermented *gueuze* beer with onions and prunes *(lapin à la gueuze/konijn met pruimen)*, as well rich pheasant *(faisan/fazant)*, venison *(biche/ree)* and wild boar *(sanglier/everzwijn)* dishes in thick sauces.

Vegetables and Salads

You will find Brabant chicory *(chicon/witloof)*, also known here as endive, and the humble Brussels sprout. Mechelen asparagus is notable equally for its taste and for its price. Meat forces its way into some local salads, particularly in Wallonia, as in *salade liégeoise*, a mixture of smoked bacon, potatoes, onion, parsley and green beans.

Although the Belgian diet is dominated by meat and fish it is not too difficult to adhere to a varied vegetarian regime. Dedicated vegetarian restaurants are thin on the ground (and full vegan restaurants just about non-existent), however, so you'll have to rely on the handful of vegetarian options that many eateries include on their menu, or on mixing and matching accompaniments and side-dishes. Ethnic restaurants, like Italian and Italian, are more likely to have meat-free dishes.

Cheese

There are more than 300 varieties of Belgian cheese (*fromage/kaas*), and the country has no strong objection to sampling cheeses from France, Holland, England (Belgium even produces its own 'Gouda' and 'cheddar'). Most local champions, such as Château d'Arville, Corsendonk, Le Regalou, Passendale, Petrus, Rubens and Wynendale are craft cheeses. Cheeses produced by Trappist monks, such as Chimay, Maredsous and Orval are greatly appreciated. Meals traditionally end with a selection of cheeses, so leave some room for them if they are on the menu.

A fine setting for a meal in Oudenaarde

Desserts, Pâtisseries and Fruit

Belgians love a good dessert, and the more chocolate and cream it contains, the better. Ice cream *(glace/ijs)* and whipped cream *(chantilly/slagroom)* are usually involved, perhaps oozing from pancakes or waffles. A *dame blanche* – vanilla ice cream and hot chocolate sauce – is an ideal way to round off a meal. The choice in cakes, fruit tarts, pastries, buns and biscuits is large. Classics include spicy *speculoos* biscuits from Brussels, *kletskoppen* (butter biscuits from Bruges) and *baisers de Malmédy* (meringues filled with whipped cream).

Specialisation of the regions also extends to fruit. The Overijse district east of Brussels produces excellent table grapes, and the Haspengouw district yet further east is good orchard country, producing mainly apples (and apple juice) and pears. Strawberries are a speciality of the Wépion district along the River Meuse.

Drinks

Beer *(see box on page 104)* is to the Belgians what wine is to the French, and *genièvre/jenever* (gin) is what malt whisky is to the Scots. Most of the wine drunk is imported from France, Germany and Luxembourg, but usually you can expect to find a wine or two on the list from Italy, the US, Chile and other countries.

Coffee *(café/koffie)* is fairly strong and usually served with extras such as little biscuits or chocolates. Tea *(thé/thee)* is often served in a glass, with a slice of lemon and without milk. Herbal teas are widely available.

> The stiff grain-spirit commonly called *genièvre/jenever* (gin) is known in Flanders as a *witteke* and in Wallonia as *pèkèt*. Belgium produces 270 varieties at 70 distilleries. Each one has a distinctive taste and some are flavoured with juniper, coriander and other herbs and spices.

To Help You Order...

Could we have a table?	Est-ce qu'on peut avoir une table?
	Heeft uw een tafel voor ons?
I'd like...	Je voudrais.../Ik wil graag...
The bill, please	L'addition, s'il vous plaît
	De rekening, alstublieft

bread	**pain/brood**	pepper	**poivre/peper**
butter	**beurre/boter**	potatoes	**pommes de terre/**
coffee	**café/koffie**		**aardappelen**
dessert	**dessert/nagerecht**	salad	**salade/sla**
fish	**poisson/vis**	salt	**sel/zout**
fruit	**fruit/vrucht**	sandwich	**sandwich/boterham**
ice cream	**glace/ijs**	soup	**potage/soep**
meat	**viande/vlees**	sugar	**sucre/suiker**
menu	**carte/menukaart**	tea	**thé/thee**
milk	**lait/melk**	wine	**vin/wijn**

...and Read the Menu

agneau/		**haricots/bonen**	beans
lamsvlees	lamb	**jambon/ham**	ham
ail/knoflook	garlic	**lapin/konijn**	rabbit
ananas/ananas	pineapple	**langoustines/**	
anguille/paling	eel	**langoestinen**	prawns
cabillaud/		**légumes/**	
kabeljauw	cod	**groenten**	vegetables
champignons/		**moules/**	
champignons	mushrooms	**mosselen**	mussels
côtelette/cotelet	chop	**oeuf/eier**	egg
crabe/kreeft	crab	**oignon/ui**	onion
crevettes/		**olives/olijven**	olives
garnalen	shrimps	**pêche/perzik**	peach
cuit à l'eau/		**petits pois/**	
gekookt	boiled	**erwten**	peas

dessert/ nagerecht	dessert	poisson/vis	fish
dinde/kalkoen	turkey	pomme/appel	apple
filet/filet	fillet	porc/varkensvlees	pork
fraises/ aardbeien	strawberries	poulet/kip	chicken
		raisins/druiven	grapes
framboises/ frambosen	raspberries	ragoût/gestoofd	stewed
		ragoût/stoofpot	stew
fromage/kaas	cheese	riz/rijst	rice
fruits de mer/ schaaldieren	shellfish	sauce/saus	sauce
		saucisse/worst	sausage
gâteau/cake	cake	sole/zeetong	sole
glace/ijs	ice cream	steak/biefstuk	steak
		veau/kalfsvlees	veal

Belgian Beer

Belgium has more than 500 different beer varieties. Many of these are craft products served in distinctive glasses, the speciality of a region, town or village. Others, including Stella Artois, Jupiler and Maes, are plain but palatable pils beers. Most bars stock at least a dozen or two (most of them in bottles), and a few have more than 100. Those on tap (*bière de pression/bier van het vat* – or you can ask colloquially for *une chope/een pintje*) are cheaper than the bottled variety.

Brussels' sweet *gueuze* beer is fermented without yeast; *kriek* is flavoured with cherries; and *faro* with candy sugar. Antwerp's dark De Koninck is yeasty. Duvel (Devil) is a gold-coloured, refermented brew. The potent Kwak is served in a bulbous glass supported by a wooden frame. A white beer *(bière blanche/witbier)*, such as Hoegaarden, Brugse Tarwebier, Dentergems and Blanche de Namur, is wheat-based, honey-coloured, cloudy and slightly bittersweet, and is often served with a slice of lemon.

Trappist monks provide Belgium with heavenly beers, including Chimay, Grimbergen, Maredsous and Orval.

HANDY TRAVEL TIPS

An A–Z Summary of Practical Information

A

ACCOMMODATION (see also CAMPING, YOUTH HOSTELS and the list of Recommended Hotels on page 129)

Local tourist offices can provide lists of hotels in their area with descriptions of facilities and prices. They can also book rooms for you on payment of a deposit, which is deducted from your hotel bill. If you arrive without a room, try this service first.

Tourist offices also have lists of local bed-and-breakfast accommodation, and in some country areas of accommodation on farms and in properties of character called *gîtes* and *chambres d'hôtes* in Wallonia; in Flanders, this concept is known as *plattelandstoerisme* (countryside tourism) and you might stay in a centuries-old *kasteelhoeve* (manor-farm).

Hotels are rated from one to five stars, based on their facilities, a rating indicated on a blue badge on the hotel's front door. The number of stars is not always a reliable guide to a hotel's quality. Some four-star hotels may have certain facilities yet still be unpleasant, while hotels further down the scale don't offer those facilities yet can be delightful. Some hotel exteriors and foyers look splendid, but this can be deceptive. It makes sense to inspect a room before taking it. At the bottom end of the scale, below one star, are two letter-ratings: H for plain hotels and O for hotels that meet only the minimum legal standards.

A substantial breakfast is often included in the room rate. If you have to pay extra for breakfast, it's usually wise to do so, even if you are on a tight budget, as it might enable you to skip lunch.

High season is generally July and August, plus the Easter, Christmas and New Year holidays. Bruges, a popular tourist destination, is particularly busy in the summer months and at weekends. Brussels' more business-oriented hotels, on the other hand, are generally busiest on weekdays and from autumn to spring; at other times, business hotels in particular may offer good discounts. Hotels on the coast are certain to be busy during the summer; those in the Ardennes are busy at this time too but may also experience a surge during the autumn game season and the winter ski season. It is always advisable to book in advance, but some kind of hotel accommodation is almost certain to be available, even at peak times, though it may not be your ideal choice.

Do you have a single/ double room?	**Avez-vous une chambre pour une/deux personnes?**
	Hebt u een eenpersoonskamer/ tweepersoonskamer?
with bath/shower?	**avec bain/douche**
	met een bad/douche
What's the rate per night?	**Quel est le prix pour une nuit?**
	Hoeveel kost het per nacht?

AIRPORT *(aéroport/luchthaven)*

Brussels National Airport <www.brusselsairport.be>, at Zaventem, 14km (9 miles) northeast of the centre of Brussels, is Belgium's main international airport and is served by many major airlines. Following the demise in 2001 of the Belgian national flag carrier Sabena, other airlines, including SN Brussels Airlines, have taken over many of its routes. The airport has all the currency exchange, shopping and eating facilities you expect at an international airport. There are good bus and train connections to Brussels (journey time to the centre is about 20 minutes), and from there good train connections to most points in the country. Buses go direct from the airport to Antwerp, Ghent, Liège and Charleroi. Taxis are plentiful outside the terminal building. For flight information from within Belgium, tel: (0900) 70 000.

Some low-cost European airlines fly to Brussels-Charleroi and Antwerp airports. The airports at Liège and Ostend (Oostende) are used mainly for limited charter and commuter-type services.

Where can I get a taxi?	**Où puis-je trouver un taxi?**
	Waar kan ik een taxi nemen?
How much is it to Brussels city centre?	**Combien coûte la course jusqu'au centre de Bruxelles?**
	Hoeveel kost het naar het centrum van Brussel?
Does this bus go to Brussels?	**Ce bus va-t-il à Bruxelles?**
	Gaat die bus naar Brussel?

B

BICYCLE HIRE

Bicycles can be hired from several sources. These include many railway stations, particularly those in scenic country areas such as the Ardennes and the Kempen, at the coast, and in tourism-oriented towns like Bruges and Ghent; a discount is available on presentation of a valid train ticket. Bikes can be hired at one station and left at another. In addition, there are rental shops. Brussels, Antwerp, Liège and some other large towns are positively dangerous for cyclists. Special bicycle-lanes exist in some parts of Flanders.

I'd like to hire a bicycle	**Je voudrais louer un vélo**
	Ik zou graag een fiets huren

BUDGETING FOR YOUR TRIP

The cost of getting to Belgium from the UK and Ireland by air varies enormously. Going with Ryanair one-way from various airports in both countries to Brussels-Charleroi can cost as little as a few pounds or euros (plus taxes), but £10–£30 (€16–48) is probably nearer the average. These rates have forced carriers such as BA, BMi, Virgin Express, Aer Lingus and SN Brussels Airlines to cut their own fares.

Of the other options, going by bus from London is likely to be the cheapest. By train, Eurostar from London to Brussels offers good excursion and advance-purchase deals, as does the Channel Tunnel car-transporter. The cost of going by ferry varies depending on the route, whether travelling as a foot passenger or with a car, and whether a cabin is desired. For a foot passenger, the price varies from about £30 one way on short crossings to about £100 on long crossings.

Similarly the cost of transatlantic flights from North America varies greatly (particularly given the uncertainties of post-9/11 and bankruptcies among US carriers). A ticket from a consolidator (bucketshop), or on a special offer, might still be as low as $500 return.

For a double room with bathroom and breakfast, you can pay less than €50, but for reasonable comfort and facilities, €75 is a more realistic starting point; a mid-range hotel will cost from €75–150; and expensive hotels begin at €150. What you get varies with the location and the time of year. There's a world of difference in prices between Bruges in high season and the Ardennes in low season.

You can eat well in many Belgian restaurants for less than €25 per person for a three-course meal without wine; in mid-range establishments, you can expect to pay €25–50; and in expensive places, above €50.

Car hire is €60–80 per day for a small car.

Public museums range in admission price from rare free places to about €2.50–5 for an adult. Privately owned attractions may be more expensive, though rarely more than €10. There are invariably reduced rates for children, and often for seniors and students, too.

C

CAMPING

Camping is particularly popular in the Ardennes and the Kempen, and at the coast. Campsites are graded from one to four stars, and amenities run the gamut from basic, to almost-luxurious in recreation areas that have restaurants, bars, pools, amusement centres, bicycle-hire and more. Local tourist offices have details of sites in their areas and a leaflet giving general camping information. It is advisable to book in advance during the high season. Spending the night in cars, caravans, mobile homes and tents by the side of the road, in woods, dunes and on the beach, is prohibited.

Is there a campsite near here?	**Y a-t-il un camping à proximité?**
	Is er een kampeerterrein hier in de buurt?
May we camp here?	**Pouvons-nous camper ici?**
	Mogen wij hier kamperen?

CAR HIRE *(location de voiture/autoverhuur;* see also DRIVING and BUDGETING FOR YOUR TRIP)

There are a lot of local car hire companies, so if time permits you should compare their prices with those of the big international car hire firms. Tourist offices can provide information on car hire companies in their area, and companies can also be found in the *Pages d'Or/Gouden Gids* (Yellow Pages) telephone directory. Credit cards are the preferred method of payment, and you need your driver's licence and passport (but don't leave them with the company). Many hotels have arrangements with car hire companies that make

I'd like to rent a car	**Je voudrais louer une voiture**
	Ik zou graag een auto huren.
now/tomorrow	**tout de suite/demain**
	nu/morgen
for one day/one week	**pour une journée/une semaine**
	voor een dag/een week

it simple to arrange for a car, but a small extra charge will normally be made for delivery to your hotel. The minimum age can be 20 or 25, depending on the company and the vehicle.

The main international car-hire companies have desks at Brussels National Airport and in most main towns. Central contact numbers for these companies are: **Avis** (02) 720 09 44; **Budget** (02) 753 21 70; **Europcar** (02) 721 05 92; **Hertz** (02) 716 92 30.

CLIMATE

Belgium's climate is temperate and much influenced by its proximity to the sea, an influence that diminishes the further inland you go until, in the low mountains along the German border in the east, the climate becomes sub-Alpine. The finest weather is between April and October. July and August can be quite hot, but rain is probable even then. Winters range from mild to severe, with snowfalls common in the Ardennes, though temperatures rarely fall below freezing for long. Approximate average monthly temperatures in Brussels are:

	J	F	M	A	M	J	J	A	S	O	N	D
°C	5	6	10	13	19	21	23	22	20	14	8	6
°F	41	43	50	55	66	70	74	72	68	57	46	43

CLOTHING

The mild but unpredictable climate means you should be prepared for rain at any time of the year. A rainproof jacket or coat is advisable and an umbrella is a useful accessory. In March and April, the weather can be bright and reasonably warm, but probably interspersed with bouts of cold wind, so taking a warm coat or jacket is a good idea. In winter, heavy coats and pullovers are essential. In summer, there'll be plenty of opportunities to wear light and skimpy clothing, and at the beach a bikini or swimming trunks – but keep in mind the earlier injunction about rain. Wear comfortable shoes for sightseeing in the cobbled streets of towns such as Bruges and Ghent, and a pair of hiking boots might come in handy in the Ardennes. For going out in the evening, clothing is generally smartly relaxed and informal, even for visits to the opera, but expensive restaurants generally expect male visitors to wear a tie.

CRIME AND SAFETY (see also EMERGENCIES and POLICE)

Crime is unlikely to be a worry for visitors to Belgium, but it does exist, and is to an extent a growing problem in some cities, including Brussels, Antwerp and Liège. Violent offences are rare but drugs-related muggings and other crimes are increasing. After dark, stay alert in Metro and railway stations, and in red-light areas; avoid deserted and poorly lit areas and stay out of city centre parks unless there are plenty of other law-abiding people around. Even in places where there is very little crime, it makes sense to take elementary precautions with cameras, bags and personal effects. Valuables should be left in your hotel safe, and nothing of value should be left visible in your car, particularly if it has foreign licence plates. Cases of theft should be reported to the police for insurance purposes.

Where's the nearest	**Où est le commissariat de police le plus proche? War is het dichtsbijzijnd politiebureau?**
I want to report a theft.	**Je veux porter plainte pour vol Ik wil graag een diefstal melden.**
My handbag/wallet/	**On m'a volé mon sac à main/mon portefeuille, mon passeport**
passport has been stolen	**Mijn handtas/geldbeurs/ paspoort is gestolen.**
Help! Thief!	**A l'Aide! Au Voleur! Hulp! Dief!**

CUSTOMS AND ENTRY REQUIREMENTS

To enter Belgium for stays of up to three months, visitors from European Union (EU) countries need only an identity card, or a passport if your home country has no identity card. Citizens of most other countries, including the US, Canada, Australia, New Zealand and South Africa must be in possession of a valid passport, and in the case of some other countries, of a visa also. Residents of Europe and North America are not subject to health requirements; residents of other countries may be and should check with the local Belgian embassy or consulate before departing for Belgium.

As Belgium belongs to the EU, free exchange of non-duty-free goods for personal use is permitted between Belgium and the UK and Ireland, and other EU countries. There are generous guideline levels of goods for personal use; visitors who bring in or take out greater quantities than these may be required to prove that the excess is for personal use.

Residents of non-EU countries may bring in 200 cigarettes or 50 cigars or 250g tobacco; 2 litres still wine; 1 litre spirits or 2 litres sparkling or fortified wine; 50g perfume; 0.25 litres eau de toilette. For residents of non-EU countries, restrictions when returning home include: **Australia** 250 cigarettes or 250g tobacco, 1 litre alcohol; **Canada** 200 cigarettes and 50 cigars and 400g tobacco; **New Zealand** 200 cigarettes, or 50 cigars, or 250g tobacco, 4.5 litres wine and beer, or 1.125 litre liquor; **South Africa** 400 cigarettes and 50 cigars and 250g tobacco, 2 litres wine and 1 litre spirits; **US** 200 cigarettes and 100 cigars or a 'reasonable amount' of tobacco.

I've nothing to declare.	**Je n'ai rien à déclarer** **Ik heb niets aan te geven.**
It's for my personal use.	**C'est pour mon usage personnel** **Het is voor mijn persoonlijk gebruik.**

Currency restrictions. There is no restriction on the amount of euros or other currencies that can be brought into or taken out of the country.

D

DRIVING (see also Car Hire)

To take your car into Belgium, you'll need:
• an international driver's licence or your own driver's licence (held for at least one year)
• car registration papers
• Green Card (this does not provide cover, but is internationally recognised proof that you have insurance; though not obligatory for EU countries, it's still useful, especially in case of an accident)
• a fire extinguisher and a red warning triangle in case of breakdown
• a national identity sticker for your car
• for right-hand-drive vehicles, headlight adapters to prevent the lights dazzling other drivers

Driving conditions. Drive on the right, pass on the left. Although you may wish to drive between towns and cities, it is unnecessary and ill-advised to drive within the big cities themselves. Driving is invariably aggressive and there are complex one-way systems and intersections to negotiate, along with trams in some cities which you are not allowed to overtake and to which you must give way.

Seat belts must be worn by both driver and passengers. The use of dipped headlights is mandatory after dusk and in poor visibility. There are stiff penalties for driving under the influence of alcohol and drugs. Some offences require payment of fines on the spot.

An important rule to remember is that drivers should normally give way to traffic approaching from the right. A yellow diamond-shaped sign with a white border indicates that drivers on main roads have the right of way; if the sign has a diagonal line through it then drivers must give way to traffic from the right.

Motorways. Belgium's motorway *(snelweg/autoroute)* network is excellent, but it and the city ring roads, especially those of Brussels and Antwerp, can get clogged at rush hour. Other main roads are generally free of traffic and weekday travelling is usually smooth. Belgium's accident record, however, is one of the worst in Europe.

Speed limits. On motorways, the limit is 120km/h (75mph); on other main roads it is 90km/h (55mph). In residential areas the speed limit drops to 50km/h (30mph) or 30km/h (18mph). In all cases, lower limits may be indicated.

Are we on the right road for…?.	**Est-ce la bonne route pour…?** **Zijn wij op de juiste weg naar …?**

Parking. There is limited street parking in city centres. Car and coach parks exist in the centres, or in the case of pedestrian-friendly towns such as Bruges, around the perimeter of the centre.

Breakdowns. Belgium's two main motoring organisations are the Touring Club de Belgique and the Royal Automobile Club de Belgique. These have reciprocal arrangements with other national motoring organisations and should be able to help you if you are a member of your own national organisation. In case of breakdown, call Touring Secours/Wegenhulp, tel: (070) 34 47 77.

There's been an accident	**Il y a eu un accident** **Er is een ongeval gebeurd.**
My car has broken down	**Ma voiture est en panne** **Mijn wagen is kapot.**

Fuel and oil. Petrol stations are plentiful and most international brands of leaded, unleaded and diesel fuel are on sale.

Road signs. International pictographs are in widespread use, but here are some written signs you may encounter:

Arrêtez-vous	Halt	Halt
Carrefour	Kruispunt	Crossroads
Virage dangereux	Gevaarlijke Bocht	Dangerous bend
Forte pente	Gevaarlijke Daling	Steep hill
Déviation	Omweg	Detour
Passage piétons	Voetganger-oversteekplaats	Crossing
Stationnement autorisé	Parkeren Toegelaten	Parking permitted
Stationnement interdit	Parkeerverbod	No parking
Prudence	Voorzichtig Rijden	Drive with care
Arrêt de bus	Bushalte	Bus stop
Stop	Stop	Stop
Sens unique	Eenrichtingverkeer	One-way
Danger	Gevaar	Danger
Serns interdit	Verboden Toegang	No entry
Serrez à droite/ à gauche/	Rechterhand/ Linkerhand Houden	Keep right/left
Impasse	Doodlopende Weg	No through road

E

ELECTRICITY

Belgium operates on 220 volts, 50Hz AC, requiring standard two-pin round continental plugs. Visitors should bring their own adaptors.

EMBASSIES

Australia: Rue Guimard 6–8, 1040 Brussels, tel: (02) 286 05 00.
Canada: Avenue de Tervuren 2, 1040 Brussels, tel: (02) 741 06 11.
Ireland: Rue Wiertz 50, 1050 Brussels, tel: (02) 235 66 76.
New Zealand: Square de Meeûs 1, 1000 Brussels, tel: (02) 512 10 40.
South Africa: Rue de la Loi 26, 1040 Brussels, tel: (02) 285 44 00.
UK: Rue Arlon 85, 1000 Brussels, tel: (02) 287 62 11.
US: Boulevard du Régent 25–27, 1000 Brussels, tel: (02) 508 21 11.

EMERGENCIES

Police	**101**
Ambulance	**100**
Fire	**100**

G

GAY AND LESBIAN TRAVELLERS

For information on Brussels and Wallonia, contact **Infor Homo,** Avenue de Roodebeek 57, Brussels, tel: (02) 733 10 24; or the gay and lesbian community centre, **Telsquels**, Rue du Marché-au-Charbon 81, Brussels, tel: (02) 512 45 87. In Flanders, contact the Holebifederatie, Kammerstraat 22, Ghent, tel: (09) 238 26 26. The age of consent for gay men is 16.

GETTING TO BELGIUM

By boat. From April to September, Hoverspeed (tel: 0130 486 5000; <www.hoverspeed.com>) has multiple daily high-speed Seacat services operating between Dover and Calais and Newhaven and Dieppe. Stena Lines <www.stenaline.co.uk> has some space for cars on its freight-ferry services from Dover and Felixstowe to Zeebrugge. P&O North Sea Ferries (tel: 0870 129 6002; <www. ponsf.com>) has daily overnight service (less frequently during winter) from Hull in northeast England to Zeebrugge. Superfast

Ferries (tel: 0870 234 0870; <www.superfast.com>) has an overnight car-ferry service from Rosyth near Edinburgh in Scotland to Zeebrugge.

By car. European motorways cross Belgium from north to south and from east to west. The E19 connects Paris, Brussels, Antwerp and Amsterdam; E40 Ostend, Bruges, Ghent, Brussels, Liège and Cologne.

By train. The routes of the primary international rail lines passing through Belgium mirror those of the motorways: Paris, Brussels, Antwerp, Amsterdam; and Ostend, Bruges, Ghent, Brussels, Liège, Cologne. Three high-speed train services cover the country and its neighbours: Eurostar connects London and Brussels through the Channel Tunnel; Thalys connects Paris, Brussels, Antwerp, Amsterdam, Bruges, Ghent, Liège and Cologne; the TGV connects Lille, and from there the rest of the French TGV network, with Brussels.

GUIDES AND TOURS (see also TOURIST INFORMATION)

The best way to tour Brussels is by bus, and both coaches and open-top double-deck buses do a circuit around the centre and to outlying areas like Bruparck. Guided tours of the district in and around the Grand-Place are conducted from the tourist office in the square.

Guided tours of Bruges are available on foot and by horse-and-carriage, but the first choice of many visitors is to go on a canal-boat tour. Boats depart from several points around the centre. Similarly, the historic centre of Ghent can be toured on foot, but tours by boat and horse-and-carriage are also available.

In addition to guided tours on foot and by bus of Antwerp city centre, there are tours by boat along the River Scheldt and of the vast Antwerp harbour. An interesting specialised tour in Liège is the Simenon Tour, which covers the childhood haunts of Georges Simenon, prolific author and creator of the fictional Paris police Inspector Maigret.

H

HEALTH AND MEDICAL CARE (see also EMERGENCIES)

Visitors from European Union countries should receive free or reduced-rate emergency medical treatment in Belgium, on presentation of a European Health Insurance Card. This can be applied for at post offices in the UK and Ireland. You may be charged for treatment and prescription medicines and can claim reimbursement for most of the cost back home. It is wise to take out private travel insurance to cover the cost of illness, accident and lost luggage. For citizens of countries outside the European Union, travel insurance is essential.

In Belgium, a pharmacy, identified by a green cross, is called a *farmacie* in French-speaking areas and an *apotheek* in Dutch-speaking areas. Pharmacies should have a list in their window of nearby all-night and weekend-duty pharmacies.

Where's the nearest pharmacy?	**Où est la pharmacie la plus proche?**
	Waar is de dichtstbijzijnde apotheek?
I need a doctor/dentist/ a hospital	**J'ai besoin d'un médecin/ un dentiste/ d'aller a l'hôpital**
	Ik heb een arts/tandarts/ ziekenhuis nodig.

HOLIDAYS

Most shops are closed on public holidays; if museums are not closed they will be operating on Sunday hours. When a holiday falls on a Saturday or Sunday, the following Monday will usually be taken off instead.

1 January	New Year's Day
1 May	Labour Day

21 July	National Day
15 August	Assumption
1 November	All Saints' Day
11 November	Armistice Day
25 December	Christmas
Moveable dates:	Easter Monday, Ascension Day, Whit Monday

L

LANGUAGE

About 60 percent of Belgians, living in the northern region of Flanders, speak Dutch. Most of the remainder, living in the southern region of Wallonia, speak French. Brussels is bilingual, with a majority of French speakers. In the east of Wallonia, along the German border, there is a small community of German speakers.

English is spoken by many and at least partially understood by virtually everybody. It often serves as a 'neutral' language between Belgians themselves. Menus may be printed in English as well as French and Dutch; if they are not, most staff will be able to explain what things are.

Road signs are in the local language of the region. Many Belgian towns have different names in French and Dutch. For instance, Brussels is *Bruxelles* in French and *Brussel* in Dutch; Bruges is *Brugge* in Dutch; Ghent is *Gent* in Dutch and *Gand* in French; Antwerp is *Antwerpen* in Dutch and *Anvers* in French; Mons is *Bergen* in Dutch; Liège is *Luik* in Dutch (and *Lüttich* to the German speakers whose provincial capital it is).

M

MAPS

Adequate maps and city plans are available free or for a small charge from most tourist offices. Bookshops sell a wide range of maps. The 1:25000-scale maps from the National Geographic Institute are excellent for hiking and other specialised purposes.

MEDIA

Newspapers and magazines. English-language newspapers and magazines are available from railway station kiosks, larger bookshops and newsstands. Expensive hotels often stock the *International Herald Tribune, Financial Times* and other quality international newspapers. An English-language weekly news and what's on magazine, *The Bulletin,* is available in Brussels and other large towns.

Have you any English? newspapers	**Avez-vous des journaux en anglais? Hebt u Engelse kranten?**

Radio and television. BBC World Service and European-based American networks can be picked up easily. Many hotels have cable television with up to 30 channels, including BBC World, Sky News, CNN International and EuroNews. Belgian and Dutch channels often show English-language films and series in the original language, with local subtitles.

MONEY

Currrency. The unit of currency in Belgium is the euro (€), divided into 100 cents. Coins in circulation are €2, €1, and 50, 20, 10, 5, 2 and 1 cents. Banknotes are €500, €200, €100, €50, €20, €10 and €5.

Exchange facilities. Generally, banks offer the best rates, followed by bureaux de change at railway stations. Bureaux de change at the airport and in the street, and hotels often exchange currency at an inferior rate, or with high commission (or both). Travellers' cheques can be cashed at these locations as long as you have your passport with you. There are currency-exchange machines at

Brussels Airport which make transactions in several currencies. Cash machines called 'Bancontact' and 'Mister Cash', which accept non-Belgian cards, are widely available.

Credit cards. Many hotels, restaurants and shops accept payment by international credit cards.

Value-added tax, service charge. A sales (value-added) tax – called TVA in French and BTW in Dutch – is imposed on most goods and

Can I pay by credit card?	**Puis-je payer par carte bancaire?**
	Mag ik met mijn kredietkaart betalen?
I want to change some pounds/dollars.	**Je voudrais changer des livres sterling/dollars.**
	Ik wil graag een paar pond/ dollar wisselen.
Can you cash a traveller's cheque?	**Changez-vous les chèques de voyage?**
	Kan ik geld voor mijn reis cheque krijgen?
Where's the nearest bank/ currency exchange office?	**Où est la banque/le bureau de change le/la plus proche?**
	Waar is de dichtstbijzijnde bank/ het dichtstbijzijnde wisselkantoor?
Is there a cash machine here?	**Y a-t-il un distributeur de billets?**
	Is er hier ergens een geldautomaat?
How much is that?	**Combien coûte ceci?**
	Hoeveel is dat?

services. Hotels, taxi drivers and most restaurants also add a service charge. Both are included in the bill. Some shops operate a tax-refund scheme for non-EU visitors: look for 'Europe Tax-Free Shopping' stickers on the window and ask the retailer for details.

O

OPENING TIMES

Banks. Monday–Friday 9am–4pm or 5pm, some close for an hour for lunch. A number of banks open on Saturday morning and until 6pm on one or two days a week.

Post offices. Monday–Friday 9.30am–12.30pm and 2–5pm. Larger post offices are also open on Saturday 9am–noon.

Shops. Generally Monday–Saturday 9am–6pm. Many smaller shops close for an hour for lunch. Late-night shopping is usually on Friday until 9pm. Most shops are closed on Sunday, except for those in popular tourist areas that are aimed mainly at the visitors, and some close on Monday.

P

POLICE (see also CRIME AND SAFETY and EMERGENCIES)

The police can be reached on the emergency 101 telephone number. Officers wear dark-blue uniforms and many of them can speak at least some English.

POST OFFICES

In addition to selling stamps and delivering letters, the Post Office provides airmail, express, registered, courier, package, taxi-post, poste-restante and other services. Red-painted letterboxes are attached to walls or poles.

A stamp for this letter postcard, please?	**Je voudrais un timbre pour cette lettre/carte postale**
	Een postzegel voor deze brief/ briefkaart, alstublieft
airmail	**par avion/luchtpost**
registered	**recommandé/aangetekend**

PUBLIC TRANSPORT

Bus. Going by bus is a good way to get around in towns and cities (tram and metro are faster in those cities that have these networks) and to points outside. It is not a good way to travel long distances – trains are faster. In remote areas (in Belgium, a relative concept) such as the Ardennes and the Kempen, the bus is likely to be the better, or sole, option, but rarely is it a quick one and, out-of-season, buses are likely to be few and far between. The De Lijn company operates regional services in Flanders; TEC does the same in Wallonia.

Metro/Tram. Brussels has a fast and efficient metro (underground train) network. Antwerp's metro system is just trams that travel underground, a system that Brussels also has to complement its metro system.

Trams exist in Brussels, Antwerp and Ghent, and are generally faster than buses, but not as fast as the metro. A fabulous fast-tram service, the Kusttram (Coast Tram), covers the entire length of Belgium's North Sea coast.

Taxis. You can wave taxis down in the street, but they don't always stop. It is better to call one or wait at one of the taxi ranks outside railway stations and major hotels, and near popular tourist areas. The tip is included in the fare, which by law has to be metered.

Train. Belgian Railways (SNCB/NMBS) operates an extensive and efficient network, both internally and internationally. Domestic services, going from the fastest to the slowest trains, are Inter-City (IC), Inter-Regional (IR) and Local (L).

Numerous reduced-rate ticket options exist, such as for return journeys made at specified periods, weekends for instance, for multiple single and return journeys, and for travel by families and by more than one person. You should ask about these before buying your ticket.

Train information. Tel: 0900 10 177 or check <www.b-rail.be>.

Where can I get a taxi?	**Où puis-je trouver un taxi?**
	Waar kan ik een taxi nemen?
What's the fare to ... ?	**Quel est le prix de la course pour…?**
	Hoeveel kost een rit naar…?
When's the next bus/ train to ...?	**A quelle heure est le prochain bus/train pour…?**
	Wanneer is de volgende bus/ trein naar…?
I want a ticket to ...	**Je voudrais un billet pour…**
	Ik wil graag een kaart naar…
single/return	**alle simple/aller-retour**
	enkele reis/retour

R

RELIGION

Belgium is predominantly Roman Catholic but Protestant churches are well represented. Brussels, Antwerp and some other large towns have mosques, synagogues and Orthodox churches, and institutions belonging to other faiths.

T

TELEPHONE

The country code for Belgium is 32. Some important area codes are: Brussels 02, Antwerp 03, Bruges 050, Ghent 09, Liège 04. If you are calling from outside Belgium, you delete the initial 0 from these area codes. Inside Belgium, you *always* need to dial the full area code, even when you are calling a number from within the same area.

To make international calls, dial 00 followed by the country code: UK 44; USA and Canada 1; Ireland 353; Australia 61; New Zealand 64, South Africa 27.

The Belgacom directory enquiries (information) numbers are: domestic, 1207 or 1307; international (in English), 1405.

Public telephones take phonecards to the value of €5, €12.50 and €25, available from post offices, railway ticket counters and news-agents. Some take coins: 10 cents, 20 cents, 50 cents and €1.

TIME ZONE

Belgium is in the Central European Time zone, which is Greenwich Mean Time (GMT) plus one hour in winter and two hours in summer (between the beginning of April and the end of October, clocks are advanced one hour). Belgium is one hour ahead of the UK and Ireland, six hours ahead of US Eastern Standard Time, and 10 hours behind Australia (Sydney).

New York	London	**Belgium**	Jo'burg	Sydney	Auckland
6am	11am	**noon**	1pm	10pm	midnight

TIPPING

Service is included in most bills, so tipping is not necessary. Never-theless, tips are still appreciated, though not always expected, by

some service personnel, particularly in places that cater to a large
number of tourists. To tip as Belgians do (when they do at all) in
restaurants, taxis and hairdressers, round up your bill to the nearest
convenient amount or leave about 5 percent. A tip of 10 percent
would be considered generous in most cases.

TOILETS

In many public toilets, 'tipping' the attendant about 25 cents (or
whatever minimum amount is posted) is mandatory. In small
cafés and restaurants, men's and women's toilets may be only
notionally separated.

| Where are the toilets? | **Où sont les toilettes?** |
| | **Waar is het W.C., alstublieft?** |

TOURIST INFORMATION

Belgium has an efficient tourist information network, with offices
at national, regional, provincial, city, district and local level, and
English-speaking staff in all but some of the smallest offices. These
provide maps and information, both free and paid-for, make hotel
bookings and arrange guided tours. Before leaving for Belgium,
visitors can contact the following:

UK. For Brussels and Wallonia: 217 Marsh Wall, London E14
9FJ, tel: (0800) 9545 245; fax: (020) 7531 0393; e-mail: <info@
belgiumtheplaceto.be>; <www.belgiumtheplaceto.be>. For Brussels and Flanders: 1a Cavendish Square, London W1G 0LD, tel:
(0906) 302 0245; brochure line: (0800) 954 5245; fax: (020) 7307
7731; e-mail: <info@visitflanders.co.uk>; <www.visitflanders.
co.uk>.

US. 780 Third Ave, Suite 1501, New York, NY 10017, tel: (212)
758 8130; fax: (212) 355 7675; e-mail: <info@visitbelgium.com>;
<www.visitbelgium.com>.

Canada. PO Box 760, Succursal NDG, Montreal, Quebec H4A 3S2, tel: (514) 484 3594; fax: (514) 489 8965; e-mail: <info@visit belgium.com>; <www.visitbelgium.com>.

Belgium. Belgian National Tourist Office, Rue du Marché-aux-Herbes 63, 1000 Brussels, tel: (02) 504 03 90; fax: (02) 504 02 70; e-mail: <info@opt.be> or <info@toerismevlaanderen.be>; <www.belgium.tourism.net> or <www.visitflanders.com>.

Where is the tourist office?	**Ou est l'office de tourisme?**
	Waar is het toeristen-bureau?

WEBSITES AND INTERNET CAFES

The official tourist office sites are good starting points for surfing through Brussels, Flanders and Wallonia. For Belgium as a whole, go to <www.visitbelgium.com>; for Brussels, <www.tib.be>; for Flanders, <www.visitflanders.com>; for Wallonia, <www.opt.be> and <www.wallonie-tourisme.be>. The best internet cafés include:

Antwerp: 2Zones, Wolstraat 15, tel : (03) 232 24 00

Bruges: The Coffee Link, Mariastraat 38, tel: (050) 34 99 73

Ghent: The Globetrotter, Kortrijksepoortstraat 180, tel: (09) 269 08 60

YOUTH HOSTELS

There are youth hostels all over Belgium, with facilities ranging from basic dormitory accommodation to double rooms with en-suite showers. Details from: Les Auberges de Jeunesse, Rue de la Sablonnière 28, 1000 Brussels, tel: (02) 219 56 76; and Vlaamse Jeugdherbergen, Van Stralenstraat 40, 2060 Antwerp, tel: (03) 232 72 18.

Recommended Hotels

Brussels has all the hotels to be expected of a major international city. The biggest proportion is in the business/diplomatic sector, a consequence being that weekends and holiday periods are generally quiet and hotels try to attract leisure visitors then with reduced rates. Antwerp, Ghent and Liège have similar hotels to Brussels, but far fewer of them. Bruges, a special case, has a large number of tourist hotels, which are particularly busy in summer and at weekends. Popular towns such as Ypres, Namur and Spa have few hotels, but there are more in their environs. The Ardennes and the coastal resorts are well-served with hotels, and with all kinds of other accommodation.

Price categories are based on the cost per night in high season of a double room with en suite bath or shower, including service charge, tax and breakfast. Rates can vary according to the season and time of week. There is often a supplement for single rooms. Most hotels offer special rates for children and do special deals during low-season periods. Room rates and room features must be indicated on a list at reception and posted in the rooms.

€€€€	above 200 euros
€€€	100–200 euros
€€	50–100 euros
€	below 50 euros

BRUSSELS

Comfort Art Hotel Siru €€ *Place Rogier 1, 1210 Brussels, tel: (02) 203 35 80, fax: (02) 203 33 03.* Aficionados of modern art should feel at home in this medium-sized hotel close to Gare du Nord. Each of the cool, efficient rooms contains a work of art – painting, sculpture or installation – on the theme of travel, by a modern Belgian artist. The attached Franco-Belgian restaurant goes in more for the traditional virtues.

Conrad Brussels €€€€ *Avenue Louise 71, 1050 Brussels, tel: (02) 542 42 42, fax: (02) 542 42 00, <www.conradhotels.com>*. Large and sprawling, this business-oriented hotel on Brussels' classiest avenue is among the most expensive in town. You get what you pay for, including oceans of white marble, a heated indoor pool, a health club and spa, and a refined French restaurant. There can be few in-room amenities the Conrad has neglected to install in its luxuriously furnished rooms.

Le Dixseptième €€ *Rue de la Madeleine 25, 1000 Brussels, tel: (02) 517 17 17, fax: (02) 502 64 24, <www.ledixseptieme.be>*. A 17th-century mansion between Gare Centrale and the Grand Place, once the Spanish ambassador's residence, now houses this graceful small hotel. The large rooms, named after Belgian painters, contain 18th-century antiques and fittings, but modern beds. There are two handsomely appointed lounges.

Les Bluets € *Rue Berckmans 124, 1060 Brussels, tel: (02) 534 39 83, fax: (02) 543 09 70*. In a townhouse from 1864 off Avenue Louise, this small, quirky – and nonsmoking – hotel, filled with antiques, is a fount of country-house charm. The feeling of staying at a rural residence extends into the rooms, which are old-fashioned and comfortable.

Métropole €€€ *Place de Brouckère 31, 1000 Brussels, tel: (02) 217 23 00, fax: (02) 218 02 20, <www.metropolehotel.be>*. The hotel's main claim to fame is style. Built in the late 19th century, it retains belle-époque graces in its public spaces, along with modern comforts in its rooms. The French L'Alban Chambon restaurant is highly regarded, as is the exquisite Café Métropole, with pavement terrace.

Mozart €–€€ *Rue du Marché-aux-Fromages 15a, 1000 Brussels, tel: (02) 502 66 61, fax: (02) 502 77 58, <www.hotel-mozart.be>*. Closer to the Grand-Place it's hard to get than this mid-sized hotel that trades luxury for access and modest cost. The surrounding streets are busy – animated, if you prefer – and can be noisy, but Mozart's music takes the edge off this in the character-rich public spaces. The wood-beamed rooms have plain modern furnishings.

Rembrandt €€ *Rue de la Concorde 42, 1050 Brussels, tel: (02) 512 71 39, fax: (02) 511 71 36, <www.hotel-rembrandt.be>*. The Rembrandt occupies a 19th-century corner house in the heart of the bourgeois commune of Ixelles. Everything about the hotel speaks of an older age, from the somewhat fussy furnishings to the slumbering cats in the front room. Yet the rooms are comfortable and bright, and the location is ideal for those who favour a good night's sleep over downtown buzz.

Sabina € *Rue du Nord 78, 1000 Brussels, tel: (02) 218 26 37, fax: (02) 219 32 39 <www.hotelsabina.be>*. In a street off Rue Royale, this small hotel in a well-maintained 19th-century townhouse has some of the attributes of a private residence. The rooms don't quite match the warmth and homeliness of the public spaces, but are quiet and tastefully modern, and some have kitchenettes.

Welcome €€ *Rue du Peuplier 5, 1000 Brussels, tel: (02) 219 95 46, fax: (02) 217 18 87, <www.hotelwelcome.com>*. This small hotel – it has just eight rooms – in a townhouse from 1896 at the Marché-aux-Poissons makes up in personal attention for what it lacks in size. Each room is individually styled on a different national theme, with antiques and ethnic fittings. The associated seafood restaurant La Truite d'Argent is among the Fish Market's best.

BRUGES

Die Swaene €€€ *Steenhouwersdijk 1, 8000 Bruges, tel: (050) 34 27 98, fax: (050) 33 66 74, <www.dieswaene.com>*. This small, romantic hotel on the Groenerei canal in the city centre has comfortable rooms elegantly furnished to a high standard. Its lounge, from 1779, used to be the Guildhall of the Tailors. The hotel also has a heated indoor pool. The restaurant serves excellent seafood and Flemish cuisine.

Egmond €€ *Minnewater 15, 8000 Bruges, tel: (050) 34 14 45, fax: (050) 34 29 40, <www.egmond.be>*. There are only eight rooms in this hotel, which occupies an 18th-century mansion with gardens beside the Minnewater Park, giving it a tranquil, country ambience. The rooms are furnished in traditional style and look out over the park.

Fevery € *Collaert Mansioenstraat 3, 8000 Bruges, tel: (050) 33 12 69, fax: (050) 33 17 91, <www.hotelfevery.be>.* A small, refurbished family hotel on a quiet side street off Langerei, near the Sint-Gilliskerk, the Fevery has modern, comfortably furnished guest rooms. Bikes are available for hire.

Relais Oud Huis Amsterdam €€ *Spiegelrei 3, 8000 Bruges, tel: (050) 34 18 10, fax: (050) 33 88 91, <www.oha.be>.* A rambling canalside building, parts of which date from the 14th century, is the setting for this fine hotel with large, ornate rooms. Those in the front have a canal view and those at the back look out on a courtyard and garden.

Romantik Pandhotel €€€ *Pandreitje 16, 8000 Bruges, tel: (050) 34 06 66, fax: (050) 34 05 56, <www.pandhotel.com>.* Old-fashioned furnishings complement modern conveniences and lend an authentic touch to the rooms in this quiet, small hotel in an 18th-century mansion near the Markt.

GHENT

Cour Saint Georges €€ *Botermarkt 2, 9000 Ghent, tel: (09) 224 24 24, fax: (09) 224 26 40, <www.courstgeorges.be>.* This marvellous, modestly priced hotel across from the Town Hall has been accepting guests since 1228. Traditional furnishings and antiques grace the rooms. Rooms in a modern annex are not as interesting as those in the old building. The restaurant shares the hotel's medieval ambience and serves good Flemish food.

Erasmus €€ *Poel 25, 9000 Ghent, tel: (09) 224 21 95, fax: (09) 233 42 41.* Each room in this small hotel in a 16th-century house is furnished differently, but antiques are common to all and they have high, oak-beamed ceilings. Some overlook a garden, and some have marble fireplaces.

Gravensteen €€–€€€ *Jan Breydelstraat 35, 9000 Ghent, tel: (09) 225 11 50, fax: (09) 225 18 50, <www.gravensteen.be>.* In an elegant, high-ceilinged mansion from 1865 near the Castle of the Counts, this small hotel combines fine modern fittings with an antique look. The rooms are comfortably furnished and some have a view of the castle.

ANTWERP

De Witte Lelie €€€ *Keizerstraat 16-18, 2000 Antwerp, tel: (03) 226 19 66, fax: (03) 234 00 19, <www.dewittelelie.be>*. This stylish boutique hotel occupies three 17th-century houses in a quiet street near the Rubenshuis. The interior is decorated in a cool modern style, with white linen sofas, Persian carpets and huge vases of flowers. It has just ten rooms, so booking ahead is essential.

Postiljon € *Blauwmoezelstraat 6, 2000 Antwerp, tel: (03) 231 75 75, fax: (03) 226 84 50*. Not all the rooms in this small hotel near the cathedral have bathrooms, which helps to account for the low rates. But the rooms are clean, well-kept and furnished in a plain, modern style.

Rubens Grote Markt €€€ *Oude Beurs 29, 2000 Antwerp, tel: (03) 222 48 48, fax: (03) 225 19 40, <www.hotelrubensantwerp.be>*. A 16th-century mansion near the Grote Markt houses this comfortable hotel, which combines classical elegance with modern furnishings. The rooms are quite large and the style is individual. Breakfast is served in the garden in summer.

Rubenshof € *Amerikalei 115–117, 2000 Antwerp, tel: (03) 237 07 89, fax: (03) 248 25 94, <www.rubenshof.be>*. Near the Royal Museum of Fine Arts, this small family hotel used to be the residence of Belgium's cardinal and has lavishly appointed public spaces. The rooms are plain but comfortable.

OSTEND

Old Flanders €–€€ *Jozef II Straat 49, 8400 Ostend, tel: (059) 80 66 03, fax: (059) 80 16 95*. Like a cosy and relaxed country house in the heart of town, this hotel has lots of antiques and rustic touches, but the furnishings in the rooms are modern. There's a characteristic Belgian bar and a restaurant serving traditional Belgian specialities.

YPRES

Old Tom € *Grote Markt 8, 8900 Ieper, tel: (057) 20 15 41, fax: (057) 21 91 20, <www.oldtom.be>*. With just nine rooms, this small, family-owned hotel in the town's central square can fill up fast. The rooms are plain but comfortable. Flemish dishes are served in the hotel's café-restaurant, which has an outdoor terrace.

LIÈGE

Bedford €€ *Quai St Léonard 36, 4000 Liège, tel: (04) 228 81 11, fax: (04) 227 45 75, <www.hotelbedford.be>*. This hotel's fine position beside the Meuse compensates to an extent for its bland architecture. Things are better inside, where the rooms are well-equipped, the public spaces well-appointed, and the in-house restaurant well-regarded.

NAMUR

Les Tanneurs €€ *Rue des Tanneries 13, 5000 Namur, tel: (081) 24 00 24, fax: (081) 24 00 25, <www.tanneurs.com>*. This character-rich hotel occupies a singular, old-world building at the angle of the Meuse and Sambre rivers. The rooms reflect its age but are handsomely decorated and have fine modern furnishings. The in-house French restaurant L'Espièglerie is popular locally.

SPA

Ambassador Hotel Bosten €€–€€ *Haasstrasse 77–81, 4700 Eupen, tel: (087) 74 08 00, fax: (087) 74 48 41*. A good base for exploring Belgium's German-speaking East Cantons and the nearby Hautes Fagnes Nature Reserve, the hotel has comfortable modern rooms and a fine French restaurant.

Hôtel la Heid des Pairs €€€ *Avenue Professor Henrijean 143, 4900 Spa, tel: (087) 77 43 46, fax: (087) 77 06 44*. A villa surrounded by a garden retains the feel of the private home it once was. The public rooms are comfortable and furnished in period style, while the guest rooms are more mixed. There's an outdoor pool.

Recommended Restaurants

Eating out is one of the country's delights. In recent years, high-end establishments have shed Michelin stars seemingly relentlessly, a fact that might signify slipping cuisine standards across the board – or just that more places are dispensing with the stuffiness that often goes with Michelin status. The fact is that it's just about impossible to eat badly in Belgium, no matter what price band you are operating within. Except for the most expensive establishments, it is rarely necessary to book ahead, though at the busiest times it is wise to arrive early to be sure of a table. Tourist menus, business lunches, menus of the day and dishes of the day are common and invariably afford good value for money. It is usually cheaper to eat at lunchtime than in the evening.

Opening hours vary depending on the nature of the place. Cafés and bars are usually open for most of the day, as are many informal restaurants. Other restaurants open for two or three hours to serve lunch, and then close until the evening. Prices are for a three-course meal, including service charge and tax but not drinks

€€€€	above 75 euros
€€€	50–75 euros
€€	25–50 euros
€	below 25 euros

BRUSSELS

Brasserie de la Roue d'Or €€ *Rue des Chapeliers 26, tel: (02) 514 25 54*. You won't find a more traditional Brussels welcome than at this Art Nouveau brasserie with marble-surfaced tables, off the Grand Place. Magritte motifs and mirrors decorate the walls and frescoes the ceiling, and hardy Belgian favourites like *stoemp* and steak-frites grace the plates, supported by a good selection of Belgian beers.

Chez Léon € *Rue des Bouchers 14–24, tel: (02) 511 14 15*. Mussels are *big* in Belgium, both literally and figuratively, and nowhere more so than at this mussels specialist near the Grand-Place, and that's been true since 1893. It's not fancy, and the approach even verges on fast-food, but there's nothing wrong with its mollusc speciality, served in a variety of ways, the most basic of which is *marinières* (steamed in a vegetable stock).

Comme Chez Soi €€€€ *Place Rouppe 23, tel: (02) 512 29 21.* If ever a restaurant was misnamed, this elegant temple of taste is it – few people, surely, can claim that the food here is just like home. Master chef Pierre Wynants produces classic French cuisine to a level that has made his name a byword in the land, and achieves this feat without being overly stuffy.

In 't Spinnekopke €€ *Place du Jardin aux Fleurs 1, tel: (02) 511 86 95.* For great traditional Belgian fare, visit 'In the Spider's Web', in a coaching inn from 1762 near the Bourse. You eat in an idiosyncratic dining room, at plain, tightly packed tables. The menu lists its hardy regional standbys in the old Brussels dialect, and the bar stocks an extensive range of Belgian beers.

L'Amadeus €€€ *Rue Veydt 13, tel: (02) 538 34 27.* In a darkly atmospheric, candlelit former sculptor's studio off Chaussée de Charleroi, this is a stylish mix of restaurant, wine bar and oyster bar. The menu features modern Belgian dishes and has vegetarian options, along with meat and fish dishes, and the Sunday brunch is a real treat. In fine weather, the courtyard-garden terrace is a great place to dine.

La Manufacture €€ *Rue Notre Dame du Sommeil 12–20, tel: (02) 502 25 25.* A beacon of good taste in a former designer leathergoods factory, in an unprepossessing neighbourhood. You dine on French-based world cuisine, amid iron pillars and exposed air ducts in the refurbished workshop, enlivened with wood floors, leather benches, polished wood, and stone tables. On sunny summer days, the shaded outdoor terrace is a good place to dine.

La Quincaillerie €€€ *Rue du Page 45, tel: (02) 533 98 33.* A leading light of the trendy tendency, this fine restaurant in the Ixelles district has transcended that label through years of excellent performance. The setting is an Art Nouveau hardware store from 1903, modishly converted to create a multi-level restaurant, with piles of wrought iron and wood panelling. Seafood, including the contents of an oyster bar, and modern Continental cuisine are all on the menu.

't Kelderke € *Grand-Place 15, tel: (02) 513 73 44.* This bustling restaurant is popular with locals and visitors alike for its consistently good food, even though it's on the touristy Grand-Place, in a 17th-century, brick-arched cellar. You dine on traditional Belgian fare in a warm and convivial atmosphere at closely packed, plain tables, and the food is served from an open kitchen. Steamed Zeeland mussels are a speciality.

BRUGES

Breidel-De Coninck €€ *Breidelstraat 24, tel: (050) 33 97 46.* In the street that connects the Burg and the Markt, this long-standing exponent of the Belgian obsession with mussels has traditional style and wood-beamed ceilings. It serves the multifaceted mollusc in a wide variety of ways – the most popular of which is the basic big steaming potful – and all are worth going back for again and again. Other seafood dishes, such as lobster and eels, also feature on the menu.

De Stove €€ *Kleine Sint-Amandsstraat 4, tel: (050) 33 78 35.* A small and intimate corner restaurant, simply decorated, which looks charming when candlelit at night. It specialises in Flemish dishes, with an emphasis on seafood and steaks.

De Visscherie €€€ *Vismarkt 8, tel: (050) 33 02 12.* No prizes for guessing that a restaurant called 'The Fishery' and located in the Fish Market would have fish, and other seafood, as its speciality. In its light, breezy setting, it puts fresh North Sea produce on the plate to a high standard.

Den Gouden Harynck €€€ *Groeninge 25, tel: (050) 33 76 37.* An exceptionally fine restaurant in a brick building that was once a fish shop, 'The Golden Herring'. They serve *nouvelle* Flemish cuisine, and the wine list is superb.

Kasteel Minnewater €€ *Minnewater 4 (near the Begijnhof), tel: (050) 33 42 54.* It's not often you can dine in a château without feeling a certain stuffiness emanating from the very walls. This one does a fair job of maintaining the necessary graces, but in a democratic ambience. The Belgian and French cuisine is unpretentious and not overpriced, and the view on the Minnewater lake is superb.

Lotus € *Wapenmakersstraat 5, tel: (050) 33 10 78.* A cool, unpreachy purveyor of vegetarian cuisine, for lunch only, Lotus has an emphasis on freshness and quality that should appeal to non-vegetarians too. The choice is rather limited – very nearly to take it or leave it – with just two dishes, offered in small, medium and large portions.

GHENT

Brasserie Pakhuis €€ *Schuurkenstraat 4 (off Veldstraat), tel: (09) 223 55 55.* Amid a lively ambience in the setting of a beautifully restored 19th-century warehouse, Pakhuis serves a wide range of modern Flemish and Franco-Italian dishes. Oyster and seafood platters are a speciality.

Jan Breydel €€€ *Jan Breydelstraat 10, tel: (09) 225 62 87.* Seafood and traditional Flemish dishes are served at this polished restaurant in a side street close to the Castle of the Counts. It has a view across the canals and a small garden, and in summer you can dine outdoors.

Keizershof €€ *Vrijdagmarkt 47, tel: (09) 223 44 46.* Situated on Ghent's lively market square, this large, rambling restaurant has enough space that even when full it doesn't seem crowded. Diners pile into hearty portions of Belgian and Continental food, surrounded by a decor of wooden ceiling beams, plain wood tables and fashionably tattered walls. In summer, there are tables for outdoor eating in the courtyard.

ANTWERP

De Kleine Zavel €€ *Stoofstraat 2, tel: (03) 231 96 91.* This restaurant has a somewhat distressed look, strewn with abandoned beer crates and furnished with bare wooden tables. But don't let that discourage you. The chef-owner Carlo Didden is one of the city's most talented chefs, serving up perfectly-cooked duck, lamb and scampi.

Pottenbrug €€ *Minderbroedersrui 38, tel: (03) 231 51 47.* This seductive French-style bistro in the heart of Antwerp has been wooing locals for more than 30 years. The new owners have introduced some creative touches to the traditional French Mediterranean menu, ensuring that the place continues to attract a mixed crowd of locals and tourists.

Rooden Hoed €€ *Oude Koornmarkt 25, tel: (03) 233 28 44.* Reputed to be Antwerp's oldest restaurant, this 250-year-old establishment situated near the cathedral provides hearty quantities of regional Belgian and French dishes, some of them old standbys and some modern.

Sir Anthony Van Dijck €€–€€€ *Oude Koornmarkt 16, tel: (03) 231 61 70.* Occupying a superb location in the restored 16th-century Vlaeykensgang courtyard, this modern French-Flemish restaurant is a labour of love for its owner/chef, who removed himself from Michelin-star stress to do something that was more to his liking. The result is a relaxed experience and truly memorable cuisine.

OSTEND

David Dewaele €€ *Visserskaai 39, tel: (059) 70 42 26.* One of the most consistently excellent seafood restaurants in this coastal town, with a nautical-themed decor and fish that comes fresh from the market across the street. Ostend sole, North Sea shrimps and bouillabaisse are complemented by Mediterranean seafood and a few French meat dishes.

James Taverne € *James Ensor Galerij 34, tel: (059) 70 52 45*. At this cosy, traditional Flemish tavern, named after the Anglo-Belgian and Ostend-resident expressionist artist James Ensor, a great delicacy is shrimp croquettes. Caught by the tavern's own boat and cooked in seawater while still aboard, the North Sea shrimps taste great. You'll find the restaurant situated in an Art Deco shopping mall.

YPRES

Ter Posterie € *Rijselsestraat 57, tel: (057) 20 05 80*. Tucked away down a narrow alley off Arthur Merghelynckstraat, this rustic cafe-restaurant offers a taste of old Flanders. Traditional regional dishes can be accompanied by one (or more) of no fewer than 250 different Belgian beers, including the local Poperings Hommelbier. There's a courtyard where you can dine and imbibe outdoors in good weather.

LIÈGE

Mamé Ví Cou €€ *Rue de la Wache 9, tel: (04) 223 71 81*. The name elicits sniggers among those who speak Belgium's Walloon dialect, for its somewhat risqué reference to a female posterior, but here the traditional Walloon specialities – delicacies such as black pudding with acid cherries, and pig's kidneys flamed in Pekèt (gin) – served in this character-rich restaurant generate only admiration from the diners.

NAMUR

Brasserie Henry €€ *Place St Aubin 3, tel: (081) 22 02 04*. For all its Franco-Walloon leanings, this lively, brass-and-wood-bedecked brasserie located right beside the neoclassical cathedral has a place on its menu for Flemish specialities, including asparagus and *waterzooï* (a delicious soup-like stew). It attracts a clientele looking for a more modern style than is common elsewhere in this riverside town. The outdoor terrace at the back is a good place to dine when the weather is warm.

DURBUY

Le Sanglier des Ardennes €€€ *Rue Comte Théodule d'Ursel 14, tel: (086) 21 32 62.* The character-filled restaurant of the like-named hotel in this picture-postcard village attracts food lovers from far and wide. Continental cuisine with a French foundation is the starting point, but many of the dishes and ingredients are from the local area, including the river trout, the smoked Ardennes ham, and the game when in season. You can dine outdoors when the weather is fine.

SPA

Brasserie du Grand Maur €€ *Rue Xhrouet 41, tel: (087) 77 36 16.* A graceful 18th-century building near the Pouhon Pierre le Grand is the setting for a restaurant with an eclectic variety of French and Belgian regional specialities and seafood dishes. Lobster, oysters and sole are seafood highlights, and side of lamb and duck-liver pâté on the meat side. In good weather you can eat outside in the garden.

EUPEN

Fiasko €€ *Bergstrasse 28, tel: (087) 55 25 50.* Tucked into a corner of a tiny square in the centre of town, this sophisticated but unpretentious little restaurant, in a room with wooden beams and brick walls, serves well-considered Continental dishes. You can follow seasonally changing trends, such as during the autumn game season, but also find standbys like steak and even a worthwhile spaghetti on the menu.

MONS

Devos €€–€€ *Rue de la Coupe 7, tel: (065) 35 13 35.* In an atmospheric courtyard located just off the Grand-Place, this exceptional restaurant has a reputation around the country for the quality of its French regional dishes and Belgian specialities, including meat cooked in beer.

INDEX